GERMAN FEDERALISM TODAY

Edited by
Charlie Jeffery and Peter Savigear

Leicester University Press
Leicester and London

© The Editor and contributors 1991

First published in Great Britain in 1991 by Leicester University Press (a division of Pinter Publishers Ltd)

Editorial offices
Fielding Johnson Building, University of Leicester
University Road, Leicester, LE1 7RH

Trade and other enquiries
25 Floral Street, London, WC2E 9DS

British Library Cataloguing in Publication Data
A CIP cataloguing record for this book is available from the British Library

ISBN 0-7185-1362-2

Typeset by Florencetype Ltd, Kewstoke, Avon
Printed and bound in Great Britain by
Billings and Son Ltd, Worcester

Contents

Notes on the contributors

Philip Blair is an administrator in the Secretariat General of the Council of Europe, Strasbourg, France.

Simon Bulmer is Senior Lecturer in the Department of Government at the University of Manchester, England.

Rudolf Hrbek is Professor in the Institut für Politikwissenschaft at the Eberhard-Karls-Universität Tübingen, the Federal Republic of Germany.

Charlie Jeffery is Deputy Director of the Centre for Federal Studies at the University of Leicester, England.

Nevil Johnson is Nuffield Reader in the Comparative Study of Institutions and Fellow of Nuffield College, Oxford, England.

Hartmut Klatt is Director of Public Relations Services at the Bundestag, Bonn, the Federal Republic of Germany.

Uwe Leonardy is Ministerialrat in the Lower Saxon Mission to the Federation, Bonn, the Federal Republic of Germany.

Peter Savigear is Senior Lecturer in the Department of Politics at the University of Leicester, England.

Ronald L. Watts is Director of the Institute of Intergovernmental Relations at Queen's University, Kingston, Ontario, Canada.

Series editor's preface

The present volume is the third in the series *Studies in Federalism* published by the Centre for Federal Studies at the University of Leicester. The first volume, entitled *Federalism and Nationalism*, examined the record and the potential of federalism as a means of reconciling ethnic diversity with political unity. This was followed by a volume on *Canadian Federalism: Past, Present and Future*, which studied the evolution of a federal system which has been very significantly moulded by the pressures of ethnic and cultural rivalry. Now, in the third volume, the series moves away from the issue of federalism in its relationship to ethnic diversity and investigates the workings of a federal system in a country, West Germany, marked by a high level of ethnic and cultural homogeneity. The extension of the federal system of West Germany to include the land and people of East Germany, will not significantly alter this underlying ethnic homogeniety, though it has, as Uwe Leonardy stresses in the final chapter of the book, sharply intensified the economic heterogeneity or inequality within the system. The federal system now incorporates, even more comprehensively than before, a single German nation in the ethnic and cultural sense.

The rationale of federalism in contemporary Germany is hence not primarily that of protecting or guaranteeing ethnic diversity, though the example of Bavaria in particular should make us careful not to discount this factor entirely. When one looks back to the making of the West German Basic Law in 1948–9, it is clear that the adoption of a federal system of government owed as much to the ineluctable situation in which the nascent state found itself as it did to the free choice of the people. Pressure exerted by the allied occupying powers for a decentralised system, and the fact that political structures in the western part of Germany had been built up from regional bases in the period from 1945 to 1948, made it fairly certain that the new constitution would be a federal one. Nonetheless there was also a significant degree of support expressed at that time by Germans themselves for a federal system, and the root of this support seems to have been a sense that federalism, by dispersing power territorially, makes its abuse less likely, and serves as a barrier against the excesses of democracy. Federalism, in other words, was seen as an adjunct or correlative of a liberal system of government in which checks and balances help to protect the liberty of the individual. Like liberalism, it appealed strongly to many who had experienced twelve years of plebiscitary dictatorship. More recently, in East Germany, federalism doubtless found support for much the same reasons.

The close link between federalism and liberalism is of course not the only distinctive feature of the German system. Those who framed the new constitution in 1948–9 had a rich, indigenous tradition of federalism to draw upon and to learn from. Although popular commentators on Germany's political past tend often to ignore the fact, the German-speaking areas of Europe have always been *par excellence* the areas in which confederal or federal forms of government have flourished within the continent. Moreover in the course of its evolution the Germanic tradition of federalism has developed organisational principles that differ significantly from those that characterise the American federal system and indeed those federal systems, such as the Canadian and the Austrialian, which blend the British notion of responsible government with American-type structures. The post-war German federation incorporates some of these distinctive organisational principles, and it is one of the main purposes of the pages that follow to provide a full account of the way they have operated in practice. Gone are the days when K.C. Wheare could dismiss virtually the whole Germanic experience of federalism, past and present, as not providing authentic examples of 'federal government'. The need now is to grasp the nature of this distinctive model and to assess carefully its strengths and weaknesses.

This need has become all the more more pressing with the development of European integration. Even in its present form the European Community has some interesting points of resemblance with the German federal system, and it is possible that the resemblance will grow stronger in the years ahead. For example, one of the distinctive features of the German federal system is that the division of power between the centre and the member units coincides to a large extent with the division between law-making and law-application. In other words, much of the legislation passed by the federal government is administered by the officials of the *Lander*. In the European Community this division of functions between the central institutions and the member states is also apparent and is likely to remain a permanent feature of its evolving structure.

Perhaps even more significant is the way the Council of Ministers of the European Community resembles the *Bundesrat*. The latter is, as the pages that follow amply testify, the central pillar of the German federal system. It brings together members of the governments of the *Länder* and gives them a share in the legislative process. It thus differs radically from the American Senate which was composed originally of deputies chosen by the legislatures of the member states, and is now composed of deputies chosen by the people of the several states. Like the *Bundesrat*, the Council of Ministers of the Community is an intergovernmental legislative body, though it differs from it in that its meetings are not public.

There has been a strong tendency amongst those who write about the Community to see a complete antithesis between the idea of 'inter-governmentalism' and the idea of 'supranationalism' or 'federalism'. The German example shows with particular clarity that this antithesis is an error. Intergovernmentalism in Germany is a constitutionally recognised and integral part of federalism.

The study of German federalism is hence not only of interest in its own right, in so far as it illuminates the political system of a country of great and growing significance in world affairs; it is also of interest because of its relevance to the process of creating a 'closer union' among the peoples of Europe.

Murray Forsyth
Series editor

Acknowledgements

This volume of essays grew out of the conference 'Forty Years of West German Federalism', which was held at the Centre for Federal Studies, University of Leicester, in September 1989. The Editors would like to express their thanks to the Anglo-German Foundation and the Nuffield Foundation for the generous financial support which enabled the conference to take place.

Introduction

Charlie Jeffery and Peter Savigear

A severe test faces Germany and the German peoples as the two states which were created after 1945 consolidate their union. In some respects the greatest challenge is the process of constitutional adjustment necessary for the incorporation of the German Democratic Republic into the existing framework of the Federal Republic of Germany. This is therefore a moment of trial for the Federal Constitution of 1949. The framers of the Basic Law had always envisaged a time when a unification of Germany would take place. That time has come. However, during the last four decades of West German federalism, many of the practices and procedures within the federal system have been honed into set patterns familiar to electorate, elected representatives and administrators alike. These must now adjust and bend to a new union of German *Länder*, expanded by the incorporation of the GDR. How will the constitutional realities of the Federal Republic stand up to the changes which have arisen since the breach of the Berlin Wall on 9 November 1989 and the quite striking speed of the drive towards unification throughout 1990? This book offers insights into these problems of adaptation by providing an analysis of the constitutional basis upon which the process of unification is taking place.

The chapters in this volume grew out of a conference held at Leicester University in September 1989 to commemorate the fortieth anniversary of the 1949 Federal Constitution. The papers presented at the conference therefore preceded the dramatic events which have taken place since November of that year. Despite this, the chapters presented here have maintained, if not increased their relevance. The aim was to probe the special nature of West German federalism, in particular its constitutional and institutional structures. The chapters thus explore both the working practice as well as the principles and form of the German federation, focusing on areas of controversy, problems peculiar to the German experience and the directions in which the federal system has evolved since 1949. These issues have become all the more important under the impact of impending unification. The expansion of the German federal system will inevitably intensify existing tendencies and problems, and bring new ones to the fore. This volume provides pointers as to how these problems and tendencies may be manifested in day-to-day practice and how the federal system can flex and adapt to accommodate them. The process of unification has been widely considered since November 1989 from the financial and economic angle. Indeed, it has often been presented as an essentially economic matter. The result has been a neglect of the problems of constitutional and institutional adaptation. With its emphasis on these aspects of contemporary German politics, this volume offers a contribution to a more balanced and rounded debate.

In many ways the present federal system is the culmination of a long period of searching for a single constitutional formula which can unite and contain the German peoples. The struggle for unity in the past, the experiments with so many different political forms, the rejection of centralism and the brief and catastrophic aberration of centralised, unitary government between 1933 and 1945 are, as Nevil Johnson shows in the first chapter of this volume, all entwined with a long tradition in Germany favouring decentralised, territorial politics. In this sense, the Basic Law of 1949 is wholly consistent with German political traditions and, for this reason, along with its very real practical success and resilience over the last four decades, it offers a uniquely promising formula for a smooth and satisfactory process of unification, able to embrace even a formerly centralised entity such as the GDR.

However, as Ronald Watts makes clear in his chapter, the traditions favouring decentralised government which are embodied in the Basic Law are not founded upon the need, underlying other federal constitutions, to accommodate regional disparities arising either from the sheer geographical size of the state concerned or from clear-cut ethnic and cultural divisions. The distinctiveness of the Federal Republic lies not in its great regional diversity but in the peculiar constitutional mechanisms which create a 'horizontal' federalism. One of the key features of the constitution drawn up in 1949, and of many of its subsequent amendments, is the way in which the governments of the *Länder* have been drawn into the process of making and, in particular, implementing federal legislation. Rather than enjoying a 'vertical' distribution of competences, with legislative powers and responsibilities clearly divided between *Bund* and *Länder*, the two levels of government have become increasingly intertwined and enmeshed within the federal legislative process. This has resulted in the establishment, as Uwe Leonardy shows in Chapter 3, of a vast and complex array of committees and conferences designed to secure and institutionalise cooperation and coordination between the organs of the federal and *Länder* governments.

The scope and importance of this network of relationships between *Bund* and *Länder* has often been understated in the study of the politics of the Federal Republic. This applies in particular to the role of the *Bundesrat*. As Leonardy shows, this unique institution occupies a pivotal position in the federal system, securing the input of the *Länder* governments into the formulation and scrutiny of federal legislation and, at the same time, providing them with a platform in their role as the main administrators of federal laws. This dual role places the *Bundesrat* at the very heart of the political system of the Federal Republic. Indeed, as the concept of 'Chancellor democracy' becomes more and more inappropriate, it might now be more pertinent to consider whether '*Bundesrat* democracy' would be a more realistic characterisation of the essence of German politics as we enter the 1990s.

The sheer density and complexity of the network of coordinative machinery, with the *Bundesrat* at the very centre, wedding *Bund* and *Länder* together, does, however, raise some interesting questions about the way in which the Federal Republic functions. These questions form the focus of the chapters by Simon Bulmer and Hartmut Klatt. Bulmer argues that the permanent process of bargaining and negotiation between *Bund* and *Länder* institutions, which such a system engenders, is not always consistent with governmental efficiency or democratic accountability. The need to secure consensus in potentially protracted *Bund–Länder* negotiations can lead to decidedly unwelcome outcomes, for example, a limited speed of response to pressing problems, or the formulation of policies where the necessity of compromise produces sub-optimal solutions. Equally, the extent of bargaining which takes place, often 'behind closed doors', raises serious questions about the transparency of the system to the public eye, and thus about the level of democratic accountability contained within it.

Klatt, on the other hand, concentrates on a problem implicit in many of the other chapters in the volume. He presents an account of the gradual, apparently inexorable tendency towards the centralisation of the German federal system. Although the governments of the *Länder* have been increasingly drawn in to the federal legislative process, this has often reflected the dilution of the autonomy of the *Länder* legislatures. Areas of legislative responsibility originally allocated exclusively to the *Länder* in the Basic Law have gradually been either usurped wholly by the *Bund*, or have become subject to the 'cooperative' federalism of *Bund–Länder* negotiation and coordination as outlined above. This has especially been the case since the late 1960s, as successive periods of economic recession have heightened the need for national economic and budgetary policy coordination. As a result, areas of social and economic policy, which were originally the concern of the *Länder*, have become subject more and more to joint *Bund–Länder* policy formulation in the quest to attain national economic objectives. This trend has been intensified by the difficulties of certain of the *Länder*, particularly those facing concentrated problems of structural industrial decline, in generating the resources necessary for the fulfilment of their constitutional functions. Once again, the *Bund* has stepped in, contributing further to enmeshment of *Bund* and *Länder* activities and accelerating the process of centralisation.

Another factor promoting centralisation, and a particularly strong threat to the autonomy of the *Länder*, is the process of European integration. This threat is manifested in two ways. On the one hand, the federal government, through its representatives in the Council of Ministers, is deeply involved in the process of formulating European Community legislation directly applicable in the Federal Republic. The *Länder* have no such direct input into a legislative process which inevitably affects their interests. On the other hand, and following from this, areas of policy which have traditionally been the responsibility of the *Länder* are now increasingly (particularly under the terms of the Single European Act) matters of EC jurisdiction. However, as Rudolf Hrbek shows in Chapter 5, the organs of the *Länder* – primarily the *Länder* governments – are striking back with some success by seeking both to extend and institutionalise their input into the EC policy of the federal government and to improve their access to the decision-making machinery in Brussels.

However, on balance it cannot be denied, despite the relative success of the *Länder* in defending their interests in EC matters, that the long-term trend is one of centralisation. While not all commentators would agree wholly with Klatt's assertion in Chapter 7 that 'behind the federal façade, a largely unitary and centralised state form has been established in the Federal Republic', it is indisputable that the range of policy areas in which the *Länder* exercise sole or primary jurisdiction has progressively diminished since 1949.

Moreover, it is almost inevitable that this trend towards centralisation will continue unabated in the process of German unification. This can be seen most immediately in the prominent role taken by Helmut Kohl since November 1989 and in the intergovernmental negotiations led by Kohl and his East German counterpart, Lothar de Mazière, preceding the all-German elections of December 1990. Although the West German *Länder* have by no means been fully marginalised in this process, it is clear that major, far-reaching policy decisions, with massive implications for the *Länder*, have been taken with only limited *Länder* participation.

It is also clear that the incorporation of the GDR into the Federal Republic will create major new problems of policy coordination in the coming years. The economic and technological backwardness and the relative poverty of the newly incorporated territory will generate the need for new, or at least expanded institutions and mechanisms of policy coordination, particularly in the areas of wealth redistribution and economic restructuring. Unification will thus intensify the practice of 'cooperative' federalism and accelerate the process through which federal and *Länder* governments are becoming ever more enmeshed. This will tend to concentrate decision-making even more at the federal level. Although the *Länder* governments will remain embedded in this federal decision-making process, it is difficult not to conclude that increased *Bund–Länder* coordination will result in a further diminishment of the already very limited number of policy areas for which the *Länder* exercise legislative responsibility.

A further consolidation of the centralising trend which has almost always been apparent throughout the history of the Federal Republic is likely to arise from the fact that the new *Länder* established in the eastern regions of Germany will, for some years at least, be financially incapable of fulfilling the functions assigned them by the Basic Law. It was noted above that several of the incomparably more prosperous West German *Länder* have become increasingly reliant on federal aid in this respect. It follows then that the incorporation of several impoverished East German *Länder* will result in massive extra financial intervention – and all the political leverage this brings with it – by the *Bund*. Moreover, in the coming years East Germany will be a prime candidate for aid from the Regional and Social Funds of the EC. Once again, this will favour the *Bund* at the expense of the *Länder*, given the limited input of the *Länder* into the decision-making machinery of the EC. All in all, it would seem then that the process of unification will add significantly to the centralising momentum within the Federal Republic, pushing it closer to Klatt's vision of a centralised, unitary state. However, as Uwe Leonardy shows in Chapter 8 of this volume, this is a scenario of which the *Länder* are aware and which they are concerned to counter. From November 1989 onwards, they have taken steps to ensure their influence over the deliberations and decisions of the federal government concerning unification. They have also sought to establish links with, and dispense aid to, the nascent *Länder* of East Germany, thus securing some influence over the East German input into the unification process and establishing, at least potentially, some sense of solidarity with the emergent East German *Länder*, no doubt with one eye on future *Bund–Länder* negotiations in united Germany.

Unification is therefore highly likely to consolidate the centralising trend in the Federal Republic. It is also likely to exacerbate the problems noted by Bulmer in Chapter 6 of maintaining governmental efficiency and democratic accountability in a 'horizontal' federal system characterised by a high degree of intergovernmental negotiations and coordination between *Bund* and *Länder*. The addition of several East German *Länder* to the federation will further increase the complexity of the thicket of *Bund–Länder* coordinative bodies at the same time as the increased need for policy coordination following the incorporation of the GDR will complicate and expand their agendas. This does not bode well either for the maintenance of existing levels of 'efficiency' or for the transparency and accountability of the system to the electorate.

One solution to such problems, examined by Leonardy in Chapter 8, would be to undertake a reorganisation and rationalisation of the *Länder* community. The creation of larger (and therefore less) *Länder*, more equal in terms of resources, would simplify and 'unclog' the system, allow for greater openness and enable the *Länder* to fulfil their constitutional functions more adequately. However, such fundamental changes would raise the thorny question of constitutional amendment. Indeed, the process of unification will inevitably require a whole range of amendments to the Basic Law. Such major constitutional reform will place new burdens and responsibilities on the Federal Constitutional Court, particularly as *Bund* and *Länder* attempt to defend their interests *vis-à-vis* each other under these new constitutional norms. As Philip Blair shows in his chapter, the Federal Constitutional Court has an established record of arbitrating between *Bund* and *Länder* over issues of constitutional interpretation and controversy. Moreover, it has tended, on the whole, to defend the prerogatives of the *Länder* against the encroachment of the *Bund*. With the extra centralising impetus unification will generate, the role of the Court as 'referee' of *Bund–Länder* relations will become a key factor in German politics in the coming years.

Many of the issues which are raised in this volume will be resolved or bypassed by events as the political structures and procedures of unified Germany take on an ever firmer shape. Much of what is discussed here is likely to change in some way. However, the underlying nature of the German federal system has to be understood in order to perceive the significance of these changes and developments. Such an understanding is offered in this volume. Inevitably, it has not been possible to consider in depth some of the more specialised aspects of German federalism. For example, there is only limited coverage of the fiscal arrangements which lubricate the system.[1] Similarly, specific problems of public policy are approached only tangentially.[2] The way in which Berlin fits into the federal structure – bearing in mind its potential future status as capital and *Land* – is barely treated. These are all important matters for future study and analysis. But they all require a precise grasp of the nature of the federal system which has emerged in Germany during the past four decades.

One message from these chapters is clear: the strength of the constitution of the Federal Republic lies in the institutions of the *Länder* and their relations with the *Bund*. It is not enough to know about the Chancellor and the *Bundestag* to claim an understanding of modern Germany. Perhaps the most intriguing aspect of the process of unification is the way in which the established network of *Bund–Länder* relations adapts and reacts to a new political scenario. The West German *Länder* have already made plain their interest in assisting the process of unification and defending their role in the new constitutional and political practice of united Germany. However, as Leonardy warns in the final chapter of this volume, it may, in the last resort, be the *Bund* which enhances its political power in this fascinating period of political change.

Notes

1. For an up-to-date evaluation of this topic, see Rüdiger Voigt, 'Financing the German federal system in the 1980's', in *Publius. The Journal of Federalism*, **19** (1989), 99–114.
2. An excellent analysis of the West German policy process is provided in Simon Bulmer (ed.), *The changing agenda of West German public policy*, Association for the Study of German Politics/Dartmouth, Aldershot (1989).

Territory and power: some historical determinants of the constitutional structure of the Federal Republic of Germany

1

Nevil Johnson

Introduction

There are three countries in Western Europe which, constitutionally, are federations: Switzerland, Austria and West Germany. Of these West Germany – or to give it its correct designation, the Federal Republic of Germany – is by a wide margin the largest in population, the strongest economically, and politically the most influential both within Western Europe and more widely in the world at large.

Those states in Western Europe which are federations constitute in important respects exceptions to what has widely been regarded as the normal pattern of European political development, that is to say evolution towards a more or less unified nation-state. In the case of Germany there was for centuries awareness of German language, culture and nationality. But for complex reasons it never proved possible to establish a political organisation coinciding with the boundaries of language and nationality. Instead, German political development was characterised by the division and subdivision of sovereignties within the bounds of what were often loosely called the German lands. Until modern times Germany contained within itself many states of different size, character and constitution: what it did not experience was the unified and centralised nation-state. Instead, the achievement of something like national unity in 1871 came about only through recognition of the peculiarities of Germany's past: a federal structure was for different reasons regarded as necessary and expedient by the principal political interests involved.

West Germany is, however, of interest to students of federal forms of government for more than historical reasons. More clearly than any other country it exemplifies a federal structure based on different principles from that of the United States. American federalism can be characterised as vertical, by which we mean that the states constituting the union have original powers enabling them to legislate independently in respect of matters not explicitly entrusted to the Congress.[1] There is in the American federation a thorough-going duality of jurisdictions which leaves each level of government – state and federal – acting directly on persons and property. In principle at least the relationships which exist between the federal or national level and the states are 'vertical'. In contrast German federalism is horizontal and functional. Subject to a limited concession to the concept of rights reserved to the states (which are no longer called states any way, but *Länder*), the German federal structure rests on the allocation of most legislative powers to the federal or national authorities, and of most executive or administrative responsibilities to the members of the federation, the *Länder*. The two levels (and the two sets of powers) are tied together through the rights of the *Bundesrat*, the Federal Council representing the *Land* Governments, in the passage of federal (i.e. national) legislation. Thus the pattern of relationships within the system of government is predominantly horizontal: there are federal institutions which determine the framework of public law (as well as exercising important powers on behalf of the federation as a whole), and there are state or provincial institutions which implement much of the policy determined at the federal level.[2]

Quite obviously a federal structure of this kind -- which has, moreover, become firmly established and has a reputation for success in operation – can and does accommodate different kinds of relationship between the central political interests and structures on the one hand, and the component parts of the federation on the other. Moreover, within and between the *Länder* there are many manifestations of what is often now referred to as 'territorial politics'. But if we turn our attention to the historical foundations of the German federal structure, what are now fashionably called centre–periphery relations were largely irrelevant to the re-establishment in 1949 of a federal system. Indeed, consideration of the history of the Federal Republic may demonstrate the risks of distorting the past by projecting into it contemporary perceptions which were not then at all important for those engaged in political action. We shall try to support this view in respect of centre–periphery relations, often seen as the relations between rich heartlands and poor fringes, showing that as conceived in relatively large and unified states they have little significance in West Germany. In contrast, however, it will also be argued that there is a notion of territorial politics at work which has always been a decisive component of the German federal tradition and remains so to this day. This is the idea that the political importance of individuals or parties is likely to be a function of the prestige, influence and support they enjoy in a particular territory. The wider society is seen as divided up into fiefdoms, as it were, and such social realities have mediated and qualified the sense of national unity and political unification.

The historical foundations of federation in Germany

Why does West Germany have a federal structure? After all, compared with the United States or India, it is a small country. It now has an ethnically homogeneous population, common cultural and linguistic traditions, a highly developed and integrated economy, good communications, and a pattern of organised party political interests reflecting for the most part national rather than local or regional concerns. To answer this question one has to go back to history, first to the long sweep of modern German political evolution, and secondly to the particular circumstances in which the Federal Republic was established in 1948–9.

In Western Europe Germany stands out as a society which achieved political unification late and on unusual terms. As has already been noted, until political unification in 1871 (and incomplete unification at that) Germany consisted of a patchwork of states varying from large territorial units such as Prussia to city states such as Hamburg. Its experience was entirely that of territorial politics in the sense that political power in the geographical area known as Germany was distributed amongst authorities of differing weight and importance, most of them dynastic in character, but some ecclesiastical and a few republican. How powerful such authorities were depended, broadly speaking, on the strength and resources of their territorial bases as well as on external factors such as foreign intervention and ambition. It is a familiar fact that from the mid-seventeenth century onwards the House of Hohenzollern understood best how to extend and consolidate its territory and thus to increase its power in relation to the other territorial units in the old German empire. This was how Brandenburg-Prussia emerged as a major European state.[3] In pursuing this policy the Hohenzollerns were, of course, following the example of their rivals, the House of Habsburg who, though German and ruling over German territories, extended the ambit of their authority chiefly by the accretion of non-German territories, thus acquiring a polyglot empire in which the German elements were in fact a minority despite their predominance in its administration. During the nineteenth century some recognition of territorial politics in the sense referred to in the introduction became a condition of survival for the Habsburg empire. Territorial politics was thus by no means a purely German phenomenon, but became a familiar experience throughout central Europe.

The ubiquity of territorial politics in the history of Germany before unification necessarily had the consequence that there was no centre. As a result of this fact the picture which most Germans have of their past differs profoundly from the historical images familiar in Britain, France or Spain where there is a long experience of government from a dominant capital city. There has been no single all-pervasive centre in the German political evolution. Instead there was a plurality of 'centres', some of them larger, more prosperous and more durable than others, and many of them forming the core of what generally became absolutist states. After 1871 it appeared for a time that Berlin would become the unchallenged political and commercial centre in the new German Empire. But that turned out to be an interlude and the events of the period 1933–45 were to confirm that there would after all be no dominant centre such as can be found in most neighbouring countries. Logically, of course, the absence of a centre renders problematical the concept of peripheries. At best in the German case it can be held that there were in the past a number of 'centres' which had a certain awareness of territories somewhat remote from them which had to be held attached, occasionally by concessions to their specific interests. Yet all this is is a far cry from the socio-economic context of contemporary Western Europe in which the distinction between centre and periphery generally reflects the belief that areas peripheral to the centre are disadvantaged by neglect on the part of that centre. This is a state of affairs for which there is no substantial foundation either in earlier German history or in the experience of the Federal Republic.

When political unification was achieved in Germany it was on unusual terms. It came about essentially through the achievement of hegemony by a single large state, Prussia. This involved the exclusion first of Austria-Hungary and then of France from effective intervention in German internal affairs, and the bringing together of the German states into a confederation under the leadership of the Prussian monarchy. However, the policy pursued so masterfully by Bismarck after 1862 was intended just as much to preserve Prussia as a dynastic state as to satisfy German national demands by bringing about a measure of political unification. This duality of purposes was clearly expressed in the initial step towards unification, the North German Confederation of 1867 and then, more dramatically, in the Empire formed in 1871. This was a federation of states (twenty-five in all) in which the decisive role of Prussia was recognised through its dominant position in the institution which was formally sovereign, the *Bundesrat*, or chamber representing the governments of the member states. Yet the *Reich* as constructed in

1871 also allowed the other states to retain considerable internal autonomy in the administration of domestic policies and services.

No centralised governmental and administrative structure for the *Reich* was established, though there were several *Reich* agencies and after 1871 the sphere of *Reich* administrative responsibility did expand and rapidly gained more importance, not least as a result of the process of legal unification which went ahead, and of the growth in specific *Reich* services. Nevertheless, it remained characteristic of German administrative federalism under the Empire that the central *Reich* authorities could for the most part supervise the growing unification of public services with the aid of quite small central agencies. This was practicable because legal developments in Germany had already resulted in a sophisticated body of public law which embodied such a strong sense of the rationality and necessity of common, general conditions that decentralised administration presented few serious risks of fragmentation or capricious variation.

Of substantial importance was the fact that the political principles on which the Empire was constructed were backward-looking and at odds with the then prevalent movement in Europe towards parliamentary forms of government. This circumstance did, however, qualify the consolidation of the *Reich* as a nation-state. It worked against the strengthening of national political organisations and tended to preserve particularisms which stood in the way of centralising tendencies in the system of government. Furthermore, although the *Reich* Government steadily grew in importance (and to some extent this occurred because the offices of *Reich* Chancellor and Minister-President of Prussia were as a rule held in personal union and their responsibilities overlapped), *Reich* representative political institutions remained weak. The *Reichstag* failed in the period 1871–1918 to achieve a system of responsible government and thus to become the focus of political life. In consequence political parties remained excluded from effective responsibility. Such factors had an important retarding effect on the consolidation of the nation state in Germany. Finally, it is necessary to remember that the political unification of 1871 was in national terms incomplete, leaving outside the *Reich* large German populations, chiefly in the Habsburg empire. This was to have disastrous effects in the years after 1919.

The nemesis of the nation-state 1919–45

The federal structure which was re-established in 1949 has distinct similarities with that of 1871, particularly in respect of the position of the *Bundesrat* in the system, and of the horizontal division of powers between the national legislature and the states, with the latter chiefly responsible for the administration of laws and policies determined centrally. But the Federal Republic also owes much to the example of the Weimar Republic, notably in relation to what can loosely be called the democratic components of its constitution. Nevertheless, the Weimar constitution did weaken the federal elements in the structure of the German state, strengthening the *Reich* authorities at the expense of the states or *Länder*. The constitutional bias against federalism was then reinforced by the political conflicts and economic upheavals of the Weimar period. This resulted in a marked drift of power to the *Reich* Government, particularly in the final stages of the Weimar Republic when the *Reich* Government ruled extensively by decree. In addition, there was the unresolved problem of territorial imbalance in the federal structure resulting from the preponderant size of Prussia.[4] With three-fifths of the population Prussia constituted a powerful state within the state and towards the end political differences prompted arbitrary interventions by the *Reich* Government against the Prussian authorities. When the fate of the Weimar Republic was finally sealed in early 1933 by the appointment of Hitler as *Reich* Chancellor, something much more like a centralised state was already in existence. Thereafter came the radical, yet extemporised centralisation of the Nazi regime. For twelve years, Germany had its only experience of highly centralised rule with Berlin as the centre from which radiated the powers of an arbitrary and capricious government. How far that government could in fact ensure that its orders were followed is a matter which cannot be pursued here: it was centralisation, but of a makeshift kind which to some extent allowed party potentates to rule their fiefdoms as they saw fit.

The disasters of the Nazi period and of the Second World War were followed sooner than many had imagined possible by a political reconstruction leading to the founding of the Federal Republic. The *Reich*, deprived of its sovereignty, lost virtually all its non-German populations and territories and was divided into Western and Soviet spheres of control. Prussia was formally dissolved by decision of all the occupying powers in 1947 (perhaps a unique example of the abolition of a state by formal decree). Consequent on the increasing gulf between the Western powers and the Soviet Union, it was only in the Western zones of the former German state that something like an autonomous German political reconstruction could take place. Anxious to reduce the burdens of occupation and to secure West German support for their resistance to Soviet threats, the three Western powers were by 1948 ready to envisage the re-establishment of a German state within the area they administered. Accordingly the West Germans were asked – in accordance with the decisions of the London Conference in early 1948 – to prepare a constitution for the three Western zones. By August 1948 a preliminary draft was ready (the product of the Herrenchiemsee convention) and by

March 1949 the final version was submitted to the representatives of the occupation authorities. After a certain amount of wrangling it was accepted by the Western powers, approved by all the provincial parliaments except one (the Bavarian), and promulgated. By September 1949 the Federal Republic was in business, though still subject to external tutelage. Yet within six years that tutelage was removed and the Federal Republic became a fully sovereign state. The subsequent history of its 'provisional' constitution, the Basic Law, might be held to be striking proof of the adage *'ce n'est que le provisoire qui dure'*.

The terms of reconstruction, 1948–9

What about the terms under which the reconstruction took place? The occupying powers provided instructions, but only of the most general nature. On the basis of the London conference held in June 1948, the Ministers-President of the German *Länder*[5] were presented with certain documents intended to guide them in the preparation of a constitution for the three Western zones. The key document did little more than require that the constitution to be drafted should protect individual rights, be based on democratic principles, and provide for a federal structure of government. The Western occupying powers were ready to leave the interpretation of these requirements to the constitution-making body, though reserving for themselves full rights of approval of whatever draft constitution might ultimately be submitted. As to the body which was to prepare the constitution, this was not to be a popularly elected constituent assembly or anything of that sort. Instead both the Western allies and the West German politicians preferred to build on already existing political foundations. This meant recourse to an assembly of sixty-five representatives of the *Landtage*, or provincial parliaments, which were at that time the only effective representative organs in West Germany. The Ministers-President of the *Länder* were charged with summoning such a body, which eventually received the somewhat nondescript designation of Parliamentary Council. Since there was widespread opposition to taking action which might appear to seal the division of Germany, this body was charged with producing a 'Basic Law' rather than a constitution. Naturally the Parliamentary Council reflected in its composition the strength of the political parties eligible for election to and represented in the *Landtage*.[6]

The Basic Law was drafted with remarkable speed and efficiency, mirroring to a large extent the outline provided by the preliminary Herrenchiemsee convention in August 1948.[7] There was virtually no argument at all amongst the political parties about many of the major provisions, some of which reflected a determination to avoid what were then seen as the defects of the Weimar Republic's constitution in its formulation of the conditions for a democratic system of government. It was, however, the conditions relating to the federal structure which occasioned the most heated arguments within the Parliamentary Council and, at the end, ran into some criticism from the occupying powers.

The dispute within the Parliamentary Council centred initially on the powers of the central or federal institutions as compared with those of the member states, the *Länder*. But it was never really expressed in this way, partly because nobody could in fact foresee what kind of balance would in practice be established between the central authorities and the provinces, partly because the argument was conducted in the language traditional to German federalism. This meant that it turned on the acceptance or rejection of the *Bundesrat* principle (in contrast with a directly elected Senate or some other solution) and on the determination of the powers of the *Bundesrat* should it be established. The Social Democratic Party and the Free Democratic Party leaned for somewhat different reasons towards a strong central legislative and executive authority. The Christian Democrats in the north had similar preferences on the whole, but not so the Christian Social Union in Bavaria. It was chiefly as a result of the obstinacy of the Bavarians in insisting on a strong *Bundesrat* that compromises were reached which represented far bigger concessions to the traditional *Bundesrat* principle than a clear majority in the Parliamentary Council had originally envisaged. The outcome was that the *Länder* were to remain responsible for most of the administration of services and to be joined in the central legislative process through a body made up of members of their governments.

The new *Bundesrat*, the membership of which was to reflect in a rough way the varying populations of the *Länder*, was not to have equal powers with the *Bundestag* (the popularly elected chamber), but was given a suspensive veto over ordinary legislation and a full veto only over constitutional amendments and legislation affecting the interests of the *Länder*. This latter provision was to turn out to mean far more extensive rights of veto for the *Länder* than was believed at the time it was formulated. Indeed, just over half of all legislation has as a rule had to have the consent of the *Bundesrat* on account of its bearing on the rights of the *Länder*.[8] In contrast the original legislative rights of the *Länder* were restricted essentially to education, local government and the police, though in practice they extend somewhat further owing to gaps in the list of concurrent powers and the failure of the *Bundestag* to exhaust fully its concurrent legislative rights.

Perhaps typically in the traditions of German federalism, it was the administrative arrangements for revenue collection which engendered another major argument in the Parliamentary Council's deliberations on the federal structure, and into this the occupying powers too were drawn when the draft was submitted for approval. The terms of financial settlement were left incomplete in 1949, but the principle of apportionment of national revenues clearly figured in it and was to be applied more widely later on. The fact that the administrative organisation to be set up for the collection of taxes proved so troublesome was partly due to its symbolic significance for the *Länder*, and partly because those involved appreciated well enough that a constitutionally recognised share in revenue administration would confer a substantial range of political benefits on the *Länder*. This reflected the German belief that the control of affairs in a territory can serve to buttress and strengthen political influences. So eventually agreement was reached on a pattern of financial administration which involves federal–*Länder* participation in something like a joint system of financial administration.

Characteristics of federalism under the Basic Law

The federal pattern of government established under the Basic Law expresses historical continuities and earlier experiences as well as being shaped in detail by the specific conditions under which the constitutional settlement of 1949 was worked out.

Turning first to some of the conditions prevailing in 1948–9, it is important to remember that the Basic Law was written after the *Länder* had already been established as effective political and administrative units. The three Western powers discovered even before the end of 1945 that they needed German administrative agents. In a remarkably short time all of them (with the United States as pacemaker) created within their zones provincial governments which were, in most cases, quickly legitimised by the holding of elections and the drafting of *Land* constitutions.[9] By 1948 this revived collection of provincial institutions was strong enough to support and cooperate in a bizonal administrative and political structure decided upon by the Americans and British in 1947, chiefly for the purpose of acting as an effective central body for the initial phase of economic reconstruction. The *Länder* administrations were, therefore, the only effective instruments of government at the time the Basic Law was being drafted, and on this account alone their influence on the final settlement was substantial. Interests had already begun to cluster around the *Land* governments which in general had enough self-confidence to hold out for a federalist solution.

However, another political factor pointed in a different direction. Organised party political activity also had its foundations in the *Länder*, in part because of the obstacles the allied powers originally placed in the way of party cooperation across zonal boundaries. The principal political parties did, however, quickly develop in a way which caused them to act as a counter-weight to the purely provincial claims represented by the *Land* governments. The Social Democrats (SPD) in particular were concerned with the issue of German unity, whilst even the new Christian Democratic Union in North-Rhine-Westphalia was not prepared to see itself as committed to narrow *Länder* interests. Consequently the policy of the main parties was soon shaped by the conviction that they had to look forward to some kind of German state, truncated and probably limited to the Western zones, but nevertheless definitely a German state and not a mere collection of provinces. Thus the political parties re-established or founded after 1946 did for the most part counteract in some degree the particularist tendencies of the *Länder* administrations, expressing instead what might be called the national interest and recognition of the need to find means of reconstructing the country as a single entity.[10] So the new state was fashioned out of something like a creative tension between the ruling governmental interests in pre-existing territorial components and the new political forces taking shape in them and looking towards the very different conditions of a re-established German state.

The provinces or *Länder* as re-created in 1945 and after were for the most part new in the sense that there was little historical continuity of territorial boundaries, except in the cases of Hamburg, Bremen and Bavaria. On the other hand, these new 'states' did embody within them considerable continuity with earlier territorial units and thus represented amalgamations of various regional particularisms. It was partly as a consequence of this fact and partly as a result of the early establishment of *Land* governments as the principal executive agents in the country that the apparently artificial provincial map was soon consolidated.[11] The absence in many parts of the Federal Republic of immediate historical continuity in the *Länder* was not to turn out to be a significant handicap.

Finally, it has to be remembered that the Western allies did concede very wide discretion to the Germans engaged in drafting the Basic Law. Subject to the overriding general requirements laid down, the Parliamentary Council was free to fashion a constitution according to its own judgement of how this could best be done. To some extent this occurred because the Western powers did not understand German constitutional law and traditions and so were hardly in a position to tell the Germans in detail what to do. The Americans certainly believed strongly in the virtues of federalism as a support for democracy, but refrained from pressing their model on the constitution-makers. The British were more sceptical and even inclined towards centralising solutions, but also held back from asserting their point of view, whilst the French were federalists almost entirely from motives of opportunism. These external influences were, therefore, of little real significance for the resolution of problems affecting the federal structure. Moreover, regardless of their disagreements on the details of relations between federal and provincial authorities and the distribution of competences, the German founding fathers were firmly convinced that the new state had as a matter of principle to be federal. Consequently, on this question, as on the wider issues of democracy, there was no prospect of the kind of clash on fundamentals with the Western occupying powers which would have endangered the whole enterprise of constitution-making.

The Basic Law was thus a thoroughly German constitutional document in which can immediately be discerned remarkably clear continuities with past experience of constitution-making over the previous century and longer. It is a constitution which provides for that original contribution to the design of institutions for which the Germans can claim a large share of credit, namely an intricate balance between a unified system of public law applying to the whole territory and dispersion in the exercise of executive powers. This balance has been achieved by building the provincial level of government into the national or federal legislative institutions which then provide that legal uniformity to which the Germans attach so much importance as the essential defining characteristic of a state. One decisive effect of this piece of institutional engineering was that it became necessary for parties to organise themselves and to operate on a basis which recognises and makes proper use of the dispersion of powers enshrined in the constitution.[12] In earlier periods, notably during the Weimar Republic, the parties generally failed to do this and in some cases did not even try: the difference in the Federal Republic is that the parties have learnt from past experience and adapted their structures and behaviour to the norms indicated by the constitution and the opportunities they offer for the exercise of powers and the maintenance of popular support. It is a striking testimony to the strength of the federal system re-established in 1949 that forty years later the prospect of a provincial Minister-President being or becoming Federal Chancellor (and sometimes even without ever having sat in the *Bundestag*) occasions no surprise. Indeed, the history of the Federal Republic already provides several examples of the move from heading a *Land* government to the Federal Chancellorship, the kind of movement in a political career that is inconceivable in most European states.[13]

There can be little question about the historical continuities on a longer time-span in the Federal Republic's constitutional structure. Although chiefly influenced by the grim lessons of the immediate past, those who framed the Basic Law used concepts drawn from many earlier phases of German state-building. Nor is this surprising, since what other sources could they have for the expression in constitutional law of the kind of state they hoped to establish? It is always a mistake to imagine that constitutional concepts are like suits of clothes in a department store and that we can choose whatever we fancy without regard to what we have worn before. It is previous political and legal experience which provides the vocabulary out of which solutions for current problems have to be fashioned and in which the attempt to give practical expression to loosely formulated and widely shared ideals has to be made. Thus, to quote one example, the catalogue of Basic Rights with which the Basic Law opens does not use a terminology borrowed to any significant extent from the American or French language of basic rights. Instead it echoes unmistakably the formulations first used by nineteenth-century liberals in Germany when struggling to establish written constitutions and later by the drafters of the Weimar constitution.[14]

German federalism and territorial politics

We now return briefly to the theme of relations between centres and peripheries, and to territorial politics. As will be clear, the Federal Republic has no dominant political centre nor, indeed, an undisputed economic centre. But it is also doubtful whether it has had peripheries in the sense often given to that term elsewhere. The West German economy was reconstructed on market principles which were and remain inherently inimical to the special claims of particular areas. Within a competitive order a highly integrated economic structure took shape, and the immense success of the economic reconstruction meant that regional disparities in the standard of living were greatly alleviated and steadily reduced. Additionally the diffusion of responsibilities through the federal system allowed the *Länder* substantial scope for policies aimed at stimulating their own economic development within the broad framework of a unified economy. Thus the economically weaker regions – 'the peripheries' as they might be called – were never without their advocates. Additionally, the rapid rise in national income facilitated the development of the 'social component' in the social market economy doctrine, so that by the 1970s there was an exceptionally generous pattern of social security provisions in place offering something like equal benefits to all.

A further point of some importance in the present context is the cultural and ethnic homogeneity of the country. The Federal Republic has provinces – *Länder* – and, more informally, regions, in which there survive significant variations in speech, culture, social habits and so on. But there is no part of the Federal Republic which does not perceive itself as first and foremost German. Consequently there has been no cultural basis for the political distinctiveness of peripheries – no Bretons, no South Tyroleans, no Welsh or Scots. The only recent qualification to this picture of homogeneity is the acquisition of a large immigrant population of foreign guest workers. Yet whatever problems they present, these cannot be said to arise out of peripheral location.[15]

With regard to territorial politics – the part played by territory in the distribution of political influence in a society – one of the principal effects of the Basic Law has been to establish conditions which stimulated the reinvigoration of territorial politics in that distinctive sense already referred to and familiar from German historical experience. The institutional structure for the government of the country was fashioned to ensure that executive responsibilities are tied to constitutionally recognised territories and are dispersed. This in turn has made it necessary for political parties to articulate within their own structures and patterns of activity the dispersion of powers provided for in this way. To put the matter in over-simplified terms, the political reputation of party leaders is to a large extent built up on the basis of control of and support from territory. Of course, there have been exceptions to this and it would be a mistake to underestimate the extent to which a political career can now be made at the national level and with a somewhat nominal territorial basis. Nevertheless, it remains a striking fact about political life in the Federal Republic that those who have consolidated a position of influence within a particular territory – a *Land* or even a subdivision of a *Land* – tend to endure the longest and, by virtue of their territorial support, are able to exercise decisive leverage in the distribution of public offices.[16]

The constitutional settlement of 1949 was intended to promote the dispersion of political power and to avoid what was seen as a disastrous experience of centralisation and the abuse of power after 1933. The controlling parameters within which the Federal Republic evolved after 1949 and consolidated its constitutional provisions turned out to be exceptionally favourable to the realisation, in broad terms, of the intentions of the constitution-makers. The outcome has been a polity within which political influence founded on the control of territory has not, on the whole, been acquired or exercised with divisive or fragmenting effects on the system of government and the overall structure of party political activity. The Federal Republic has become a unified state in which the component parts can and do exercise their rights without being perceived as threats to the unity of the whole.

In the wake of the political changes now in train in the other part of Germany, the German Democratic Republic, it has become all the more necessary to bear in mind the lessons to be drawn from the federalist tradition in Germany. With dramatic suddenness a prospect of political reunification emerged at the end of 1989. Regardless of when and how such a reunification might be brought about, it is virtually certain to require first a revival of *Länder* within the GDR, and then the extension of well-established federal principles and practices to the whole country. In short, there will be no return to the *Reich*, but instead a reinforcement of the federalist tradition through an enlargement of the Federal Republic of Germany.

Notes

1. A succinct exposition of this view is to be found in K.C. Wheare, *Federal government*, Oxford University Press, Oxford (1963), Chapter 1.
2. For a detailed account of the Federal Republic as a federal state, see N. Johnson, *State and government in the Federal Republic of Germany: the executive at work*, Pergamon, Oxford (1983), 117–68.
3. It should not be forgotten, however, that despite the achievements of Frederick II (1740–86) Prussia remained relatively a poor state and highly vulnerable to attacks by hostile neighbours. And for a short time after 1806, Prussia was reduced to a rump as Napoleon re-drew the map of Western Europe.
4. The problem of re-drawing the territorial map did receive careful consideration by committees of experts in the later years of the Weimar Republic, but it proved hard to reach agreement and impossible to take action.
5. In 1948 there were eleven *Länder* in the three Western zones of occupation.
6. Non-voting delegates also attended from West Berlin.
7. The comments which follow on the drafting of the Basic Law rely extensively on two standard works: J. Golay, *The founding of the Federal Republic of Germany*, University of Chicago Press, Chicago (1958); and P.H. Merkl, *The origin of the West German Republic*, Oxford University Press, New York (1963).
8. An important consequence of the fact that so much legislation requires the consent of the *Bundesrat* (i.e. is '*zustimmungsbedürftig*') is that drafts tend to be the object of negotiation with the administrative authorities and governments of the *Länder*. Such collaboration is in any case rendered necessary by the fact that the *Länder* are generally responsible for the implementation of federal legislation. This issue is dealt with in detail by Uwe Leonardy in Chapter 3 of this volume.
9. Immediately after the end of the war, federalist thinking was very popular, especially under the influence of Catholic doctrines of subsidiarity. For a while it was common to equate federalism directly with democracy and, in this way, the claims to legitimacy of the emerging political institutions in the *Länder* were enhanced. For a careful account of this early phase in political reconstruction, see M.E. Foetz-Schroeter, *Föderalistische Politik und nationale Representation 1945–1947*, Deutsche Verlagsanstalt, Stuttgart (1974). It is striking that the term 'subsidiarity' now figures prominently in discussions about the future internal evolution of the European Community.

10. This theme is developed at length and in convincing detail in Foetz-Schroeter (1974).

11. Only modest changes were made in the territorial map of the Federal Republic after 1949. The most important was the fusion of the three south-western *Länder* in 1951 to form Baden-Württemberg, a prospect already provided for specifically by the Basic Law. This reduced the number of *Länder* to nine, but this came back to ten at the beginning of 1957 with the return of the Saarland to the Federal Republic.

12. To some extent it is now even a legal requirement for parties to have an internal organisation which allows for provincial (i.e. *Land*-based) representative structures. This is provided for in the Federal Law on Parties, enacted in 1967.

13. Kurt-Georg Kiesinger, Federal Chancellor from 1966 to 1969, was previously Minister-President of Baden-Württemberg. Similarly, Willy Brandt, Chancellor from 1969 to 1974, was formerly Lord Mayor of West Berlin, and Helmut Kohl, Chancellor from late 1982, was formerly Minister-President of Rhineland-Palatinate, while the SPD's candidate for the Chancellorship in 1987, Johannes Rau, was simultaneously Minister-President of North-Rhine-Westphalia.

14. There are quite striking similarities in the formulation of certain basic rights in the constitution drawn up by the Frankfurt Parliament in 1848, that imposed by 'octroi' by Frederick William IV of Prussia in 1850, the Weimar constitution of 1919, and the Basic Law.

15. On the whole, the foreign 'guest workers' have been concentrated in the larger industrial cities of West Germany and in West Berlin. The total immigrant population exceeds four million and undoubtedly in some places its high density has resulted in major social tensions between immigrants and the local inhabitants. The dimension of colour is, however, for the most part absent, though that of religion is to some extent present, and this sometimes makes for tensions in relations with the indigenous population.

16. A familiar aspect of German political relationships is the tendency of whichever major party is in opposition in Bonn to revive its strength by building up its position in the *Länder*. Slowly the SPD did this before 1966. The CDU–CSU followed suit in 1969, and there have been signs of the same process at work after the SPD left office at national level in 1982. See G. Lehmbruch, *Parteienwettbewerb im Bundesstaat*, Kohlhammer, Stuttgart (1976).

2 West German federalism: comparative perspectives

Ronald L. Watts

Introduction

Comparisons among federations are useful, but not because their institutions are easily exportable to different situations. Indeed, rarely do institutional structures applied to different countries work in the same way. The need to adapt them to differing social, economic and political conditions invariably affects their operation. Nevertheless, comparative analyses are useful because they give insights into or draw attention to the significance of certain features in a particular political system. The ways in which similar institutions operate differently, in which different institutions operate in similar ways, and in which unique institutions or traditions affect the political processes which predominate, can help us to understand a particular federal system more clearly.

This chapter will, therefore, attempt to focus upon the similarities and differences of the Federal Republic of Germany in relation to other federations, chiefly the United States, Switzerland, Canada and Australia. It will do so in terms of five sets of comparative questions. These are: (1) the processes of federalization; (2) the social bases of federalism; (3) the institutional structure of the federations; (4) their political cultures, i.e. ideas of federalism; and (5) the functional dynamics arising from the interaction of the first four aspects. The chapter will then conclude with an examination of the lessons which Canadians in their own constitutional deliberations of the past decade have attempted to draw from the West German model.[1]

The processes of federalization

Carl Friedrich has noted that federalization may occur by either aggregation of formerly separate political units or by devolution through the granting of constitutional autonomy to political units formerly subordinate within a unitary political system or empire.[2] In this respect a simplistic contrast might be made between those federations like the United States, Switzerland and Australia which at their formation were created by aggregating distinct political units, and Canada in 1867 and the Federal Republic of Germany in 1949 which emerged from previously unitary political systems. In actual fact the situation in the latter two federations was somewhat more complex.

The creation of a British North American federation in 1867 involved elements of both devolution and aggregation. In order to overcome the difficulties, deadlocks and tensions which the formerly unitary Province of Canada had suffered since the Act of Union of 1840, it was agreed to establish a federal structure in which the French majority in Quebec and the English majority in Ontario would each have autonomy over matters of cultural and local concern. To this extent devolutionary pressures were a powerful motive for the adoption of a federal system. At the same time, economic and defence motives gave impetus to the aggregation of additional provinces through the incorporation into the new federation of the colonies in Nova Scotia and New Brunswick. Furthermore, in the early decades after federation still further provinces were added both in the east and the west. Thus the structures and processes of Canadian federalism have displayed some of the characteristics of constitutional centralization usually inherent in federations created by devolution, but these have been combined with many of the political pressures inherent in a polity attempting to aggregate distinct units.

The processes of federalization in West Germany have also been complex. While the post-1945 developments were clearly devolutionary in relation to the preceding regime, the earlier unification of Germany in the nineteenth century, as Nevil Johnson's contribution to this volume emphasizes, was a history of the aggregation of various units, and that history has had its impact not only on German ideas of federalism but also upon the character of some of the institutional structures created in 1949, particularly the *Bundesrat*. Furthermore, the constitution-making body for the Bonn Constitution itself was not a popularly elected constituent assembly but an aggregation of representatives of the *Landtage* or provincial parliaments, of the eleven *Länder* in the three Western zones of occupation.

Be that as it may, the devolutionary aspect of the process by which the Bonn Constitution was created is illustrated by the quite frequent references in the discussions at this conference to the artificiality of the boundaries of the constituent political units in 1949. In a number of cases these bore little relation to previous history. Certainly, the German *Länder* display a relative lack of ethnic distinctiveness from each other with the possible exception of Bavaria. This contrasts with the sharper linguistic and religious distinctiveness of the Swiss cantons or of Quebec in Canada. But other federations have also contained constituent units which may have appeared artificial to begin with. Nevertheless, over the course of time those units have developed their own sense of community. Many of the new American states (after the first thirteen) created in the course of westward expansion would certainly belong in this category. In Canada the provinces of Saskatchewan and Alberta created in 1905 were, as their boundary lines clearly illustrate, originally artificial constructs, but the cumulative effect of eighty years of development based on their own province-building impulses now marks them off as distinct political communities with their own historical traditions. Thus, as Canadian experience has shown, a federal structure over time institutionalizes political diversity as well as unity. One can see the same processes occurring within the Federal Republic of Germany. Just to take one example, there is the energetic *Länder*-building impetus displayed by the originally 'artificial' *Land* of Baden-Württemberg.

The social bases

W.S. Livingston in his classic work on constitutional amendment in federal systems emphasized the importance of the social basis of federalism. Indeed, he referred to federal institutions as the mere 'instrumentalities' of federal societies.[3] It would be appropriate, therefore, to raise the question whether there is a social basis for West German federalism, or whether it merely represents a federal institutional structure overlaid on a non-federal society.

From a comparative perspective one might identify four aspects for consideration: (1) the degree of territorial ethnic or religious pluralism or homogeneity; (2) the degree of economic regionalism or integration; (3) the extent of economic disparities among the constituent units; (4) the impact of the international context upon internal relations.

Among those federations where the territorial distribution of linguistic or religious groups and their concentration in constituent units is particularly notable are Switzerland, Canada (particularly in the case of Quebec), and some of the newer federations such as India and Nigeria. In such cases federalism has provided a political expression for internal ethnic and religious cleavages. While such cleavages may sharpen the character of internal territorial diversity, it should be noted that in the case of Switzerland the situation is moderated by cross-cutting cleavages since the linguistic and religious cleavages do not coincide. By contrast, in Canada the religious and linguistic cleavages have tended to reinforce each other. One should note also the tendency to political polarization in such bicommunal societies as Canada and Belgium, which contrasts with the tricommunal character of Switzerland or the multicommunal character of India and Nigeria.

There are other federations, however, such as the United States and Australia, where the constituent units are not marked by sharp ethnic cleavages. In both these federations there is more general homogeneity although there are some variations of political culture and historical tradition. The same could also be said of the nine English-speaking provinces of Canada. In this respect the Federal Republic of Germany resembles more closely the situation in the United States, Australia and nine of the ten Canadian provinces.

In terms of the degree of economic regionalization or integration, the Federal Republic of Germany, with its high degree of economic integration as a unifying factor, is clearly at one end of the spectrum among federations. As a contrast, at the other end of the spectrum is Canada with a political economy based on different staple products in different provinces, which encourages provincial governments to serve these economic interests as their own distinct client groups. This has contributed to a potent economic regionalism with its decentralizing pressures within Canada. Switzerland, Australia and the United States come somewhere in between, although (in descending order) closer to the Federal Republic of Germany on the spectrum.

A closely related factor which has an impact upon the extent of divisive attitudes within a federation is the degree of economic disparity among the constituent units. Some variation in wealth among regional units is inevitable in any federation. But significant variation may provoke intense regional resentments and undermine the sense of shared national citizenship based on a common standard of services within the federation. Furthermore, the extensive disparity has a double effect: first, it accentuates the problem of political resentment at variations in the standard of services available to citizens in different constituent units; second, it makes the resolution by methods of fiscal equalization more difficult because of the much larger intergovernmental transfers of resources required to correct the situation. In terms of the degree of regional economic disparity, the Federal Republic of Germany has benefitted from the existence of less extreme disparities than in most contemporary federations. Moreover, like Australia, Canada and Switzerland, but unlike the United States, West Germany has attempted to deal formally with the problem by a system of equalization transfers to the less wealthy constituent units. The Federal Republic of Germany is unique, however, in including among those constitutionally stipulated equalization transfers a significant element of direct horizontal transfers from the wealthier to the poorer *Länder*. The other federations employing formal equalization arrangements have relied solely on transfers from their national governments to top up the resources of their poorer states or provinces.

The international context of each federation is another factor which may affect internal relations and attitudes. A classic example has been Switzerland. With Germany, France and Italy as its neighbours there has been a long tradition of avoiding alliances which might be a source of internal disunity among its own linguistic groups. Another example is Canada. The Canadian provinces represent a string of beads along the United States border with their populations concentrated in a narrow band 100 miles wide and 500 miles long. In such a situation, not only language and economic regionalism but relations with the United States have often caused internal contention. Donald Smiley has called this the third axis of Canadian federalism.[4] By contrast, in Australia and the United States, internal regionalism has been less affected by international relations. This is explained by Australia's continental isolation, and by the United States' domination of relations with its continental neighbours.

The situation in the Federal Republic of Germany is close to that of Switzerland and Canada, since relations with its bordering neighbours have an important impact upon the *Länder*. Nowhere is this clearer than among the rising concerns about the implications which West Germany's membership in a more integrated European Community will have upon the future jurisdiction and role of the *Länder* within the Federal Republic of Germany. Indeed, there are some interesting parallels between the concerns of the *Länder* during the recent negotiations for closer European integration in 1992, which are examined in this volume by Rudolf Hrbek, and the anxieties of the provinces in Canada during the negotiations for the Canada–United States Free Trade Agreement. In both cases the governments of the constituent units were concerned to protect their own interests by playing a part in the negotiating process itself. In Canada, not only did the federal government consult the provinces extensively during the negotiations, but in the end it largely finessed the issue by managing to reach an agreement with the United States which affected provincial areas of jurisdiction only to a very limited extent. Also, just as there has been a debate in West Germany about whether closer European integration represents a threat to the future roles and autonomy of the *Länder*, so has there been a debate in Canada about whether the Canada–United States Free Trade Agreement would tip the balance within the Canadian federation in favour of the federal or provincial governments. Some have argued that because the federal government would be responsible for managing the agreement and provinces would in the long run have to comply, the Free Trade Agreement would favour the former. But others have suggested instead that this particular agreement, with its free market emphasis and limited impact on provincial areas of jurisdiction, would in fact restrict the ability of the federal government to mount national economic policies while leaving provincial powers relatively intact, thus tilting the internal balance in favour of the provinces.

The recent developments in Eastern Europe and particularly East Germany also illustrate the extent to which the international context may have an important bearing upon internal relations. The incorporation of East Germany obviously has enormous implications for the evolution of the German federal structure.

The institutional structure

The Federal Republic of Germany has the basic institutional characteristics typical of previous modern federations such as the United States, Switzerland, Canada and Australia. Without getting into the complex morass of how to define federalism, one may simply note that the Federal Republic of Germany shares with these other modern federations six institutional features in common. First, in each of these systems, there are at least two orders of government, each existing under the constitution under its own right, and each acting directly on the people. Second, there is a constitutional allocation of jurisdiction and resources to the two orders of government. Third, because overlaps in constitutional jurisdiction are unavoidable, there are provisions for 'shared rule', i.e. machinery, processes or constitutional stipulations to ensure 'federal comity'. Fourth, the composition and procedures of the central institutions are based not solely on principles of majoritarian representation, but also involve some constitutionally guaranteed representation of regional and minority views. Fifth, the constitution is not unilaterally amendable by one order of government alone, but requires the endorsement by a certain proportion of the governments or the electorates of the constituent units. Sixth, in each of these political systems there is an umpire, whether in the form of a Supreme Court, a Constitutional Court as in the Federal Republic of Germany, or in certain cases the electorate in a referendum as in Switzerland, to adjudicate constitutional disputes.

But while modern federations, including the Federal Republic of Germany, have these basic features in common, there have been many variations among federations in the precise form which these institutional features have taken. In comparative terms two institutional features of the Federal Republic of Germany are particularly noteworthy. The first is the form of the constitutional allocation of jurisdiction. There is an extensive range of functions where the *Bund* has legislative authority but the *Länder* have executive responsibility. The second is the provision made for intergovernmental cooperation and for the representation of *Länder* views on national policies through the key role played by the *Bundesrat*.

Turning first to the form of the distribution of powers between the orders of government, federations may be broadly grouped into two categories according to whether the allocation of legislative and executive authority for particular subjects coincides or is divided between different governments. In one category are the United States, Australia and Canada where generally legislative and executive responsibility for a particular area is assigned to the same government. Thus, in these federations, in constitutional terms the central governments generally have both legislative and executive responsibility for the areas of jurisdiction assigned by the constitution to them, and the states and provinces have both legislative and executive responsbility for the areas of jurisdiction assigned by the constitution to them. While this is the general pattern in these federations, one may note some qualifications. In Canada, for example, criminal law is an exception to the general pattern: the constitution assigns legislative authority to the central government but administrative authority to the provinces. Furthermore, in all three federations, but most notably the United States, central legislation often delegates responsibility for the administration of grant-in-aid programs to the states, although that is not a mandatory constitutional requirement.

By contrast, the Federal Republic of Germany and Switzerland constitutionally concentrate much of the legislative authority in their central governments while constitutionally allocating administrative authority for many of those same areas in the *Länder* and the cantons. This arrangement makes possible the combination of a high degree of legislative centralization with extensive administrative decentralization. The autonomy of the constituent units in their administrative activities is protected through the constitutional stipulation of their executive authority in these areas. A corollary of such an arrangement where legislative and executive authority over specific fields is divided between governments is the increased importance of ensuring both intergovernmental cooperation and consultation of the views of the administering governments when national legislation is being formulated.

An important factor affecting the character of intergovernmental cooperation and the expression of regional viewpoints within the institutions of national government is the form of executive–legislature relationship existing within each order of government. Broadly, federations may be categorized in terms of whether the 'separation of powers' between executive and legislature has prevailed within each order of government, or a parliamentary executive responsible to the legislature has been the arrangement within national and within state governments.

The first two modern federations, the United States and Switzerland, both incorporated the separation of powers between executive and legislature within their national and state or cantonal governments as a further expression of the principle of the diffusion of authority considered to be the essence of federalism. The difference between the two was simply that in the United States authority was concentrated in a single individual, the President or the Governor, while in Switzerland the preference was for collegial executives within each government.

A second category consists of those federations, Canada, Australia and the Federal Republic of Germany, which have combined federalism and parliamentary executives. In these federations legislative and executive authority has been fused within their national and within their state governments through making the executive directly responsible to the legislature. Canada in 1867 was the first to create this hybrid form of political system. Canada followed the American precedent of the diffusion of authority by dividing authority between central and provincial governments in its federal system, yet it incorporated within each level of government the Westminster tradition of concentrating legislative and executive authority by establishing parliamentary executives. Australia followed the Canadian precedent, as have a number of the more recent Commonwealth federations including currently India and Malaysia. The Federal Republic of Germany belongs to the general category of federations incorporating responsible parliamentary executives within the *Bund* and within the *Länder*. It has introduced some unique modifications of its own, however, which have facilitated intergovernmental cooperation and the representation of *Land* views in national policy-making.

One feature common to all the parliamentary federations, by contrast to those where there has been a separation of powers between their executives and legislatures, has been the dominance of the executives in their government and in their intergovernmental relations. Thus 'executive federalism' has become a commonplace term to describe the quasi-diplomatic character of intergovernmental relations in Canada and Australia.[5] First Ministers' Conferences in Canada and Premiers' Conferences in Australia have served as summit meetings of the national and provincial or national and state first ministers, and they have become a regular feature of intergovernmental relations in both countries. And in both federations there has been a growth in governments at both levels of ministries of specialists in intergovernmental relations. This situation contrasts sharply with the United States where, for example, in 1989 President Bush met with all the governors for only the third time in the 200 years of federal history. The two previous occasions of this rare event occurred under Teddy Roosevelt and Franklin Roosevelt. Intergovernmental relations in the United States have been typified by a more diffused and complex set of interactions. These have involved the lobbying of congressmen and congressional committees and sub-committees, and administrators from federal departments by a variety of state administrators and legislators. In terms of intergovernmental relations, the Federal Republic of Germany, like the other parliamentary federations has displayed a strong tendency to 'executive federalism'. This tendency has been further reinforced by two factors. The first is the constitutional division of legislative and executive authority between the *Bund* and the *Länder*, in many areas requiring close intergovernmental coordination. The second is the unique institution of the *Bundesrat* which gives direct representation to the governments of the *Länder* within the national Parliament.

A second feature common to most parliamentary federations, by contrast with those incorporating the separation of legislative and executive authority within their national institutions, has been the weakened expression of regional and minority views within their national institutions. By comparison with the United States and Switzerland, in Canada and Australia the opportunities for the representation of provincial, state or minority views are more limited for two reasons. First, there has been the relative political weakness of their second chambers in the national parliaments since the cabinets have been responsible to the other chambers (although the Australian Senate can on occasion exert some control if it is willing to contemplate double dissolution). Second, these federations have been marked by the prevalence of strong party discipline within the popularly elected chambers (including the Australian Senate). Here too the Federal Republic of Germany displays some of the tendencies characteristic of the other parliamentary federations, but the unique form of its parliamentary second chamber, the *Bundesrat*, has had a strongly mitigating effect. The extensive range of national legislation over which the *Bundesrat* is able to exercise a veto has, as Uwe Leonardy points out in Chapter 3 of this volume, ensured the governments of the *Länder* a powerful influence upon national policy-making, and has created a strong inducement for national governments to take into account in their legislation the views of the various *Länder*.

The comparative analysis of federations in terms of the form of the distribution of powers and of the nature of their executives suggests a typological matrix of federal categories represented by the four possible combinations depicted in Table 2.1. In terms of this comparative typology, the West German *Bundesrat* is a particularly interesting institution. It serves as an intergovernmental institution facilitating cooperation between the *Bund* and the *Länder* where the constitution for large areas assigns legislative authority to the former and executive authority to the latter. And in contrast to other parliamentary federations, the *Bundesrat* serves as a device for the effective representation of *Länder* views within

Table 2.1 Form of distribution of powers between governments

	Coincident legislative and executive authority	Extensive division of legislative and executive authority
Form of executive:		
Separation of legislature and executive	United States	Switzerland
Parliamentary fusion of legislative and executive	Canada Australia	Federal Republic of Germany

national institutions which are parliamentary in form. It is not surprising, then, that during the forty years of the operation of West German federalism, the *Bundesrat* has come to play a role more important than even that expected by the founders in 1949.

While these institutional comparisons have concentrated particularly on the form of the division of powers between governments and the form of executive–legislature relationship within constituent governments, there are other institutional features of the Federal Republic of Germany worthy of brief comparative comment. The form and role of the Constitutional Court provides a contrast with the Supreme Courts in the United States, Canada and Australia. The number of states in the West German federation, ten, is more akin to that of Canada (10) and Australia (6) than that of the United States (50) or Switzerland (26). This has undoubtedly been a factor shaping the processes of intergovernmental relations. In terms of the variation in relative size of the constituent units, the Federal Republic of Germany since 1949 is by no means unique when one notes similar variations in Canada and the United States. It is worth noting, however, that the exclusion of Prussia from participation in the federation created in 1949 enabled avoidance of some of the problems which its dominant role had created for previous German regimes. The dominance of one or two constituent units within a federation has elsewhere always tended to be a destabilizing element.

Political culture, values and ideas of federalism

Both Simon Bulmer and Uwe Leonardy draw attention in this volume to notions of democratic accountability and the degree to which federalism can be reconciled with these. Traditionally, there have been two quite different approaches to achieving political accountability. One, which might be described as the pessimistic approach, is to distrust the use of power and to control it by requiring the sharing and diffusion of power and by imposing checks and balances upon its use. This was the underlying philosophy behind the adoption both of federalism and of the separation of powers between executives and legislatures in the United States and Switzerland. The other, which might be described as the optimistic approach, is that typified by the concentration of executive and legislative authority within a single body which is directly responsible to the electorate. In its purest form the responsible cabinets and the parliamentary institutions within the unitary systems of Britain and New Zealand exemplify this approach. The parliamentary federations of Canada and Australia combine elements of both principles of accountability: they divide authority between two orders of government, but within each constituent government concentrate authority in a fused executive and legislature directly accountable to the electorate. The West German institutions appear to go further in combining elements of the two principles of accountability. While the principle of parliamentary executives has been incorporated, the inclusion of a number of checks and balances, particularly through the role of the *Bundesrat*, has made the operation of the national institutions in some respects more akin to the checks and balances and sharing of power that occur in the United States and Switzerland.

A closely related issue is the question of the degree to which the complexity and bureaucratization inherent in federalism may undermine the realization of democratic values. The concern is not unique to West Germany. Criticism of 'executive federalism', constraining the role of the legislatures and reducing the opportunities for public debate, have been widespread in Canada recently, particularly among those critical of the processes which produced the Meech Lake Accord. It is also noteworthy that among the democratic nations of the world the United States and Switzerland both rank among the lowest in voter participation in elections. Against these criticisms, however, must be balanced the relative historical stability of the modern federations. Indeed, the constitutions of the United States, Switzerland, Canada and Australia are among the longest continuously operating constitutions in the world today.

Various chapters in this volume also draw attention to the tendency toward a depoliticization of issues in West Germany. It has been suggested that support for federalism with its legalism and bureaucratization has in part been based upon a fear of reversion to the intense politicization which occurred in the 1930s and early 1940s. The fear of the divisive national impact which the politicization of issues can cause is not unique to West Germany among federations. The Swiss tradition of international neutrality was founded on the fear that taking sides in international issues would have an explosive impact on internal relations among the diverse groups composing Switzerland. In Canada, Mackenzie King survived for a long period as Prime Minister in Ottawa by avoiding controversies over internally contentious issues. Indeed, it could be argued that one of the rationales of federalism itself is to remove those contentious issues which divide the country at large from the arena of national policy-making. By leaving to the state governments the responsibility to deal with these matters each as they see fit, national dissension is reduced.

Every federation has found it necessary to strike its own particular balance between the pressures for the provision of a uniform standard of services for its citizens and for the recognition of diversity. The clash between the values of uniform treatment for all citizens within a federation and of autonomous decision-making for regionally distinctive constituent units is displayed particularly vividly in the realm of fiscal federalism. Thus the use in many federations and most notably in the United States of conditional grants to support social programs in less wealthy states has at the same time often limited the autonomy of state governments. The different balance between these two values that has been struck in different federations is exemplified by the differing proportions of unconditional as opposed to conditional transfers employed. In comparative terms the United States relies the most heavily on conditional transfers. Interestingly it is Canada and West Germany which in their arrangements for fiscal transfers have most respected the autonomy of the regional units by having a large proportion of these unconditional. That is not to say that equalization arrangements do not play a major role in these two federations in assisting poorer provinces or states, but simply to say that a larger proportion of the total transfers of fiscal resources within these two federations are made with only rudimentary, or no conditions as to their expenditure imposed upon the recipient governments.

Political processes and dynamics within federations

In comparing federations one must take account not only of the patterns of establishment, social foundations, institutions and political values, but also of the political processes and dynamics created in each federation by its own particular blend of these elements.

A particularly important aspect of these dynamics is the character and role of the political parties in each federation. In the United States and Switzerland the national parties have tended to operate as coalitions of state or cantonal parties marked by loose party discipline in their operation within the national legislatures. In such a context there is considerable opportunity for the representation and open expression of regional views in national politics. Interestingly, it is now the House of Representatives as much as or more than the Senate which performs this function in the United States. In Canada and Australia, under the impact of their parliamentary systems, the national parties are marked by much stronger discipline and by the greater dominance of their leaders. There is, consequently, less freedom for the expression of regional views, and even the Australian Senate operates primarily a party house. A further contrast is that while there is a considerable interlacing of national and state parties in the United States and Switzerland, in Canada particularly, but also in Australia, there has tended to develop a more dual system of national and provincial or state parties. In Canada the national and provincial wings of the same party operate virtually autonomously with few political leaders moving successfully from one level of government to the other.

The operation of political parties in the Federal Republic of Germany provides a particularly distinctive example. Although the institutions are parliamentary in form, the *Bundesrat* as an institution has clearly affected party dynamics in an integrative way which contrasts with the sharp dualism of national and provincial parties in Canada. The potential *Bundesrat* veto of much federal legislation has induced national parties to take an interest in *Land* elections and concerns since it is the *Länder* governments who determine the composition of the *Bundesrat* and hence the ability of national governments to get their legislation adopted. At the same time, the representation of state governments within an influential national institution has induced *Land* parties and politicians to take an interest in national issues. The resulting interpenetration of national and state parties and the frequent movement of politicians from one arena to the others has thus meant that West German political parties function in a way which in some respects resembles the marble-cake character of national and state political parties in the United States and Switzerland more than the clearly dualistic pattern in Canada and Australia, even though party discipline in West Germany is much firmer than in the United States or Switzerland.

The processes of intergovernmental relations are also an important aspect of the dynamics within any federation. As already noted in the section on institutional forms, the pattern of intergovernmental interaction in the Federal Republic of Germany resembles much more that of Canada and Australia, with the executives in both levels of government dominating these processes. But the tendency to 'executive federalism' is further reinforced in the Federal Republic of Germany by the particular form of the distribution of powers, under which for many areas of *Bund* legislative authority the *Länder* have been constitutionally assigned executive authority, and by the institution of the *Bundesrat* which provides for formal participation of the *Land* executives in a substantial area of national policy-making. The extent to which there is a tighter interlocking relationship at the core of West German federalism than in any other federation raises interesting questions about whether cooperative or competitive relationships between national and state governments within federations are more efficient in the long run. Traditionally it has been assumed that because overlapping jurisdiction within federations are unavoidable, intergovernmental consultation and cooperation are essential. Indeed, virtually every federation has seen an increase in the multitude of intergovernmental cooperative arrangements during the twentieth century. But critics have recently raised questions about the efficiency and effectiveness of cooperative federalism. In the case of West Germany, Fritz Scharpf has pointed to the problems of the 'joint-decision trap'.[6] Even in other federations, where the degree of interlocking decision-making is not as extensive, there have been efforts to reduce the extent of intergovernmental interdependence. Ronald Reagan's 'New Federalism' was one such effort. In Canada, Albert Breton, applying the concepts of economics to political relationships, has suggested that just as competition within the economic realm produces greater efficiency, so in the political arena competition between governments within federations provides more benefits for the electorate than does intergovernmental executive and bureaucratic 'collusion'.[7] Indeed, Martin Landau has argued that multiplexed federal structures are in fact more efficient than simple unitary ones.[8] It is worth considering, therefore, whether one of the real merits of federalism, messy as it may seem, may lie in fostering competition between governments to serve the interests of the electorate, rather than in interlocked governmental decision-making.

The Canadian considerations of German precedents

The Canadian federation established in 1867 has a constitution much older than that of West Germany. But given the stresses which Canadian federalism has faced during the 1970s and 1980s, it is not surprising that Canadians have looked to the experience of federations elsewhere, including that of West Germany, for lessons. Three features of the Federal Republic of Germany have attracted particular attention in Canada: (1) the *Bundesrat*, (2) the electoral system, and (3) the Constitutional Court.

The ineffectiveness of the Senate of Canada as an institution has for long been a source of calls for reform. Critics have pointed to the predominantly majoritarian character of Canada's parliamentary national institutions and to the inability of a centrally appointed Senate to express with any political legitimacy regional concerns on national issues. They have argued that this has been a major factor contributing to the stresses within Canada's federal system. In the late 1970s, many Canadian bodies, aware of the constitutional crises provoked in Australia by an elected Senate in 1975, advocated a reform of the Canadian Senate along lines similar to the West German *Bundesrat*. The governments of British Columbia and Ontario, the Quebec Liberal Party, the Canadian Bar Association, and the Pépin-Robarts Commission each advocated some variant of a House of the Provinces, a second chamber which would be composed of provincial government representatives.

By the early 1980s, however, such proposals went out of fashion. It was argued that the rationale for such an arrangement which existed in West Germany, because of the allocation to different governments of legislative and executive authority for the same subjects, did not apply in Canada with its different form of distribution of authority between governments. Others, failing to recognize the integrative influence of the *Bundesrat* upon intergovernmental relations and upon national and state political parties in West Germany, expressed fears that the representation of provincial government delegates in the central institutions would accentuate divisiveness in national deliberations. Furthermore, by the 1980s the significance of the Australian crisis of 1975 had receded in the memory of Canadians. Above all, there was a clear preference in public opinion surveys for a reform of the Senate that would give it electoral legitimacy. The current fad among advocates for Senate reform in Canada, therefore, is not for the West German model but for a 'Triple E' Senate: elected, equal provincial representation and effective. The advocates expect such a Senate to provide an alternative instrument to the current processes of 'executive federalism' for the expression of regional views on national issues. Here there appears to be a refusal to recognize the lessons of Australian experience. There, what is in effect a 'Triple E' Senate has not eradicated executive federalism, and the Senate as part of a parliamentary system has operated primarily as a party house rather than a house of state views.

During the late 1970s and early 1980s there was also considerable interest in the West German mixed electoral system involving the national election of some legislators from single member constituencies within a system with overall proportionality. This Canadian interest grew out of critiques of the existing Canadian electoral system for the House of Commons which is based on single member constituencies with candidates receiving a plurality of votes being elected. In practice this system has tended to over-represent regional plurality votes and to under-present regional minority votes in the members sent to the House of Commons in Ottawa. The net effect upon the composition of the party caucuses in Ottawa has been to over-emphasise the representation of those provinces in which a party has done well electorally and further under-represent those provinces in which a party has only a minority of votes. This tendency was particularly marked in the national elections during the two decades leading up to 1980. For example, the Trudeau government in 1980 won only two seats in the four western provinces even though their candidates had obtained a considerable number of votes in those provinces. Some scholars and the Pépin-Roberts Commission have argued that a mixed electoral system with a pro-portion of members elected by proportional representation would at least ensure each party representation from each province which would reflect more accurately the aggregate vote that it obtained in that pro-vince. Resistance to such proposals arose, however, from a deep-rooted Canadian distrust of proportional representation, and from fears that such an electoral system might condemn the country to an endless series of unstable minority governments. The impetus for changing the elec-toral system was further weakened by the 1984 federal election in which Mr Mulroney's Progressive Conservatives elected substantial numbers from every region across Canada, suggesting that electoral reform to ensure broadly based national governments was not an urgent necessity.

The model of the West German Constitutional Court has also attracted some attention in Canada. During the late 1970s Alberta, concerned about a Supreme Court whose justices were all appointed by Ottawa, included among the constitutional reforms it advocated the establishment of a Constitutional Court. These proposals did not ad-vance far, however, and more recently the Meech Lake Accord of 1987 included agreement on a proposal under which the provinces would have a role in nominating candidates for appointment to the existing Supreme Court.

These instances of consideration in Canada of West German models point to the problems which arise in any effort to transfer institutions from one country to another. Nevertheless, the study of German pre-cedents has helped Canadians to get a better insight into their own institutions and processes.

Conclusions

Two concluding points arise from this review of West German federa-lism from a comparative perspective. First, the different elements of West German federalism do display a number of similarities with various aspects of other federations, but in the Federal Republic of Germany they have been brought together in their own unique blend of institutions and processes. Second, the Federal Republic of Germany exemplifies a complexity of institutions and processes which is typical of all federations. As Alec Corry, a noted scholar of Canadian federalism, used to say: 'a neat and tidy mind is a crippling disability in efforts to understand the operation of federal systems.'

Notes

1. This is a revised version of a paper given at the conference organised by the Centre for Federal Studies, University of Leicester, in September 1989 on 'Forty Years of West German Federalism'.
2. Carl J. Friedrich, *Trends of federation in theory and practice*, Frederick A. Praeger, New York (1968), 7.
3. W.S. Livingston, *Federalism and constitutional change*, Clarendon Press, Oxford (1956), 1–15.
4. Donald V. Smiley, *Canada in question: federalism in the eighties*, 3rd edn, McGraw-Hill Ryerson Limited, Toronto (1980), 252–83.
5. Ronald L. Watts, *Executive federalism: a comparative analysis*, Institute of Intergovernmental Relations, Queen's University, Research Paper No. 26, Kingston, Ontario.
6. Fritz Scharpf, 'The joint-decision trap: lessons from German federalism and European integration', *Public Administration*, **66** (1988), 239–78. See also Simon Bulmer's contribution to this volume.
7. Albert Breton, 'Supplementary statement', Royal Commission on the Economic Union and Developmental Prospects for Canada, *Report*, Ministry of Supply and Services, Ottawa (1985), 483–526.
8. Martin Landau, 'Federalism, redundancy and system reliability', *Publius*, **3** (1973), 173–96.

The working relationships between *Bund* and *Länder* in the Federal Republic of Germany

3

Uwe Leonardy

Introduction: terms of reference

The 'classic' reply which a German receives when asking in Britain about the functions and structures of a peculiarly British institution, such as, for instance, the House of Lords, very often consists of the simple but nonetheless true observation that 'it is an odd thing, but it works'. The point being made here is certainly not to suggest that, apart from also being a second chamber, the House of Lords is in any way comparable in a practical sense with the *Bundesrat*. However, these two institutions are comparable inasmuch as they are both, in their own way and history, unique in the world. This uniqueness is reflected in the mass of litera-ture – in particular about potential reform initiatives – which floods into our libraries whenever either one of them gets embroiled in some political controversy or becomes the focus of dispute between political scientists or legal scholars writing or debating about constitutions.

In much of this writing and debating, however, the intricate details of the actual working structures, within which these institutions perform their roles as one of the basic cogwheels within the overall machinery of government, have all too often been taken for granted. Such omissions often lead to misunderstandings in evaluating their roles. In a publi-cation on German federalism, this would seem to underline the need for a predominantly descriptive chapter[1] on the working relationships be-tween the federation and its component parts, in which the *Bundesrat* is certainly the central, but in fact not the only cog which keeps the system going. This chapter will therefore discuss the working relationships, in their constitutional, political and administrative aspects, between the organisational entities which together constitute the German federal structure.

An analysis of financial working procedures and arrangements is thus ruled out as being beyond the scope of this chapter.[2] A further chapter in itself would be necessary to explain why the distribution of financial resources in West Germany ultimately results in what might rightly be termed a 'federalism by negotiation'. Nevertheless, it should be borne in mind throughout the description of the institutional network undertaken in this chapter that financial questions often fill, or at least underlie, the agendas of many of the institutions under discussion.

Also excluded from the ambit of this chapter are the various categories of legal instruments used as the tools of internal federal relationships. These range from official treaties to executive agreements between *Bund* and *Länder*, and between the *Länder* themselves, and include the various, more or less formal agreements between the Federal Chancellor and the Minister-Presidents of the *Länder* and between the Minister-Presidents themselves. It is sufficient to state that a wide variety of such tools is employed alongside the constitutional arrangements for federal legislation (including delegated legislation) by either the Federal Government or by any of the executive branches in the *Länder* authorised to do so by federal law.

Moreover, the emphasis in the chapter is on executive rather than on legislative cooperation. While stressing this aspect, however, the chapter does not wholly exclude the cooperation of the executive branches of both the federal and the *Land* levels of government in the preparation of federal legislation. Rather, it is intended to indicate that cooperation between the executive branches is more prominent in the West German system than cooperation between the legislatures of *Bund* and *Länder*.

Last but not least, with the exception of one specific reference to the election of justices of the Federal Constitutional Court by the *Bundesrat*, the organisation of the judicial branch (and in particular the recruiting of judges for other federal courts) falls outside the scope of this chapter.

The components of the institutional structure of German federalism

As in any genuinely federal form of government, there is not one single working relationship between *Bund* and *Länder* in the German system, but a multi-faceted network of such relationships, both formal and informal, bilateral and multilateral, individual and collective.

This multi-faceted network of *Bund–Länder* relations is one of the distinguishing features of the German model and reflects the peculiar division of responsibilities in the German system. One of the essential characteristics of this system is that the bulk (though of course not all) of legislation is enacted at the federal level, while the *Länder* are the main administrators, even in the field of federal legislation. This might seem paradoxical in the face of Article 30 of the Basic Law,[3] which states in general terms that 'except as otherwise provided or permitted by the Basic Law, the exercise of government powers and the discharge of governmental functions shall be incumbent on the *Länder*'. However, in the practical process of filling the statute books, this constitutional stipulation has been all but eroded in the legislative sphere by the impact of both the broadening of the criteria, and the expansion of the catalogues, of the concurrent, exclusive and framework legislative powers of the Federation, as enshrined in Articles 72–75 of the Basic Law. The progressive exemption of the bulk of legislation under these articles from the rule that 'the *Länder* shall have the right to legislate in so far as this Basic Law does not confer legislative power on the Federation' (Article 70) has only left a fairly small, though by no means unimportant, amount of legislative powers for the *Länder*.

However, this has in no way diminished the central role of the *Länder* in administering not only their own, but also federal legislation. This role is defined in Article 83 of the Basic Law, which confers upon the *Länder* both the right and the duty to 'execute federal statutes as matters of their own concern in so far as this Basic Law does not otherwise provide or permit'. In this field, whose ambit is set out in Article 84 and 85, the *Länder* are clearly the predominant bodies, while federal administrative powers, which are defined in Articles 87–90, are classed more as exceptions than as the rule.

It is this fact, then, which explains that in spite of the diminishing role of the *Länder* in the passing of legislation as such, their impact in the process of preparing federal legislation has constantly expanded rather than receded. Moreover, this fact (in conjunction with historical factors) is the underlying reason why the *Bundesrat* has always been an intergovernmental organ. However, it is by no means the only one.

While it is necessary for the purpose of explanation, it is nonetheless a hazardous undertaking to try to isolate and categorize the components of the entire network of federal institutions, because these components are all more or less always in communication with each other, and are also often linked with each other by organisational mechanisms. Bearing in mind these limitations, three levels, or areas of relationships may be discerned.

Firstly, there is the level of what might be termed the 'Whole State' (*Gesamtstaat*), i.e. the level which comprises institutions in which both the Federation (the *Bund*), and its component parts (the *Länder*) are represented on terms of equal status. This arrangement of equal status allows no room for majority decision-making. All decisions in this sphere must consequently be arrived at by accommodation and compromise, or they must be limited by 'agreement to disagree'. In addition, decisions taken in this sphere may also require approval in the federal or *Land* legislatures.

Secondly, there is the level of the 'Federal State' (*Bundesstaat*), i.e. the constitutionally organised structure of interrelationships between *Bund* and *Länder* institutions, whose decisions are subject to majority voting rules. The subject matter of all such decisions must be located within the field of federal competence, or they must be subject to federal procedures, as in the case of the 'Joint Tasks' (*Gemeinschaftsaufgaben*), in which federal participation takes place in areas of competence originally exclusive to the *Länder*,[4] and in which the Federation and the *Länder* cooperate by virtue of specific agreements.[5]

The voting procedures in all of these fields are regulated in various ways. Article 51 of the Basic Law sets out the voting rules for *Bundesrat* plenary sessions, giving three votes to *Länder* with up to two million inhabitants, four to those with up to six million and five to those with over six million. The voting rules for *Bundesrat* committee work, which grant one vote to each *Land* irrespective of the number of inhabitants, are set out in the Standing Orders of the *Bundesrat*,[6] while special federal statutes regulate voting procedures for 'Joint Tasks' (which are administered by Joint Planning Committees in which the Federation casts eleven votes and the eleven *Länder* one each).

Thirdly, there is the level of horizontal coordination between the *Länder* themselves (i.e. excluding the Federation), which in a strict sense is not part of the field of *Bund–Länder* relations, but without which neither the decisions of the 'Federal State' nor those of the 'Whole State' could be properly prepared. On this level, the agendas can consist both of federal and *Land* matters. In both fields, decisions must be unanimous and may also require approval in either the federal or *Land* legislatures. This area is also commonly known as the 'Third Level'.

The system as it stands

On the basis of this distinction between the three levels of the *Gesamtstaat*, the *Bundesstaat* and the 'Third Level', the main institutions in the working relationships between *Bund* and *Länder* are outlined below.

The Gesamtstaat

At the level of the *Gesamtstaat*, or 'Whole State', there are three main groups of coordinative and cooperative institutions. At the top, regular conferences between the Federal Chancellor and the Heads of Government of the *Länder* are held in a more or less regular sequence of roughly every two months. Their legal basis is set out in No. 31 of the Standing Orders of the Federal Government.[7] Although this rule has been part of these Standing Orders ever since the Federal Government came into existence in 1949, these conferences did not become a regular institution until Chancellor Willy Brandt took office in 1969. His predecessors, Konrad Adenauer, Kurt-Georg Kiesinger and Ludwig Erhard (in particular Adenauer) only convened these conferences in cases of more or less extraordinary or special need, because they were anxious not to let the Minister-Presidents and the Heads of the City-States interfere too much, let along regularly, in what they apparently considered to be exclusively federal business. Brandt then made these conferences a permanent part of what he rightly considered to be a structure of the 'Whole State' by including in their agendas topics on which either the Federation is dependent on the *Länder*, or on which the competences of both sides are so closely connected with one another that separate action would compromise the effectiveness of any of the parts of the system. This view, and the regular convention of these conferences which followed from it, have since been a feature of the Chancellorships of both of Brandt's successors, Helmut Schmidt and Helmut Kohl. Nowadays, it has also become a regular practice that these conferences of the Heads of Government of Federation and *Länder* are prepared and preceded by meetings of the Chief of the Chancellor's Office with his colleagues in the *Länder* (the *Chefs der Staats- und Senatskanzleien*).

Moreover, it is not only here but also in all other fields of *Bund–Länder* relations that the Chancellor's Office performs the role of the central coordinator at the federal level. This too is an innovation which dates back to Brandt's time in office. Until then, there had been a Federal Minister of Cabinet rank with particular responsibility for 'Affairs of the *Bundesrat* and the *Länder*'. These so-called '*Bundesrat* Ministries' proved, however, to be too weak and thus inadequate in performing the central task of coordination, a factor which led Brandt to entrust the Chancellor's Office with this coordinating function..

The second group of coordinative institutions comprises the top-level coordinating machineries of the political parties. Here, the relevant bodies are mainly established within specially created *Bund–Länder* structures, among them in particular the institutionalised Conferences of Party Leaders in the *Bundestag* and the *Land* Legislatures, which are partly assisted by permanent staffs. Also, the party executive committees or presidiums at the federal level, assisted by the party headquarters, play a prominent role in the handling of *Bund–Länder* business. This is especially so in the case of the CDU, where the coordination of federal–

Land matters often needs to be pre-prepared with a view to subsequent negotiations with the independent 'sister party' in Bavaria, the CSU. The impact of the CSU is so strong, particularly in constitutional questions with relevance to the federal system both in domestic and European Communities legislation, that the CSU group within the joint CDU–CSU Parliamentary Party in the *Bundestag* even has a veto right of its own in all political projects which touch upon this field.[8]

This leads to the point where the *Länder* groups of *Bundestag* members within each of the parliamentary party factions need to be mentioned. These consist of all the members of one specific party who come from one specific *Land*. Each of these groups has a chairperson of its own, and they convene regularly at intervals of one to three weeks in their *Land's* Mission to the Federation in Bonn to discuss *Bundestag* business relevant to their *Land*.

The third group of institutions in the field of the 'Whole State' is concerned more specifically with inter-parliamentary coordination. It is represented in the Conference of Parliamentary Presidents of *Bund* and *Länder*, and its more frequently convened nucleus, the Conference of Presidents of *Land* Legislatures. Like the Conferences of the Heads of Governments, these meetings are also prepared by senior officials (the directors of the parliaments).

In contrast to these three widely known groups of conferences, there is one further coordinative institution, which operates in the field of foreign relations, which has remained largely outside the public view. Its place is, so to speak, 'on the borderline' between the institutions of the 'Whole State' and the 'Federal State'. This is the Permanent Treaty Commission set up by the Agreement between the Federal Government and the Cabinet Offices of the *Länder* on the Treaty-Making Power of the Federation of 14 November 1957 (the so-called Lindau Agreement). The purpose of this body, which is composed of representatives of the *Länder* (mainly civil servants working in the *Länder* Missions in Bonn), is to receive information from, and to reach agreements with, the Foreign Ministry and other federal ministries if and whenever international treaties, whose provisions encroach partly or wholly on the exclusive legislative powers of the *Länder* or their 'essential interests', are under negotiation. In most cases, this Commission, in which representatives of the Federal Government have speaking, but not voting rights, is concerned with treaty-making in the field of cultural affairs. However, it is neither in theory nor in practice confined to this sector. Its structure and functions were later developed into the organisational model which today shapes the relations between *Bund* and *Länder* in European Community matters. This point is developed at greater length in Rudolf Hrbek's contribution to this volume.

The Bundesstaat

At the level of the *Bundesstaat*, or 'Federal State', the number of organisational units is, naturally, the greatest, and the intensity of interaction
between them is at its highest. Here, the *Bundesrat* is at the centre of the
structure. In constitutional terms and in working practice, the *Bundesrat*
is both the legislative organ of the *Länder* within the 'Federal State' and,
at the same time, the federal organ of administration in the 'Whole
State'.

This dual role has its origin in the twofold effects of Articles 50 and 84
of the Basic Law. Article 50 clearly rules that 'the *Länder* shall participate
through the *Bundesrat* in the legislation *and* administration of the federation'. Further, Article 84 states that all federal statutes which regulate
the institutional and/or procedural aspects of the role of the *Länder* in
the execution of those statutes require the consent of the *Bundesrat*. This
reflects the general responsibility of the *Länder* for the implementation
of federal legislation. Thus the role of the *Bundesrat* is a double one in a
double field: it is both a co-legislator (with the *Bundestag*) and a representative of the *Länder* in their function as the administrators of federal
legislation. Its place, therefore, is predominantly within the 'Federal
State', but also partly within the 'Whole State'. In the performance of this
combined role, it is assisted by the bodies outlined below.

All *Bundesrat* plenary business[9] is prepared in a system of highly
efficient committees which sit every third week and submit their recommendations to the plenary session which follows two weeks after the end
of the committee week. Some committees have permanent sub-
committees, such as the Sub-Committee for Construction and City
Planning set up by the Committee for Internal Affairs. Others, in
particular the Committee for Legal Affairs, frequently create *ad hoc* sub-
committees. All sub-committees report their recommendations to the
committee which created them.[10] In most cases, both committees and
sub-committees are manned by civil servants of the *Länder* (predominantly from their missions in Bonn), while federal civil servants represent the Federal Government. With the exception of the Finance
Committee and the so-called 'political' committees (Foreign Affairs,
Defence and Inter-German Relations), federal and *Länder* ministers
rarely participate personally in committee meetings unless they hold the
chair. Committee chairmanships are distributed between the *Länder* by
the *Bundesrat* in plenary session according to a pre-arranged and rarely
altered pattern.[11]

The preparation of committee and sub-committee meetings, minute-
taking and the drafting of the committees' recommendations to the
plenary sessions of the *Bundesrat* are the main tasks of the Secretariat of
the *Bundesrat*. The Secretariat is headed by a Director, who assists the

President of the *Bundesrat* in preparing for and presiding over the plenary session held on every third Friday.

The Permanent Advisory Council (*Ständiger Beirat*) formally advises the President of the *Bundesrat*. However, the President rarely participates in the weekly meetings of the Council as he is normally preoccupied by his primary function as a Minister-President or one of the Mayors of the City-States. Thus, in practice, the Council, under the chairmanship of the longest-serving member, manages the political business of the *Bundesrat* together with the Director of the Secretariat.[12] In addition, the Council has the important function of receiving regular information on Federal Cabinet meetings immediately after the Cabinet has sat every Wednesday. As a rule, this information is conveyed to the Council by the Minister of State in the Chancellor's Office in charge of *Bund–Länder* relations, or by the Chief of the Chancellor's Office (at present a minister of cabinet rank). The Council is composed of the Plenipotentiaries (*Bevollmächtigte*) of the *Länder* to the *Bund*,[13] who are in most cases (but need not necessarily be) members of their *Land* Cabinets.

If the Plenipotentiaries have not been successful in reaching agreement on the handling of any particular item of plenary business (either in the Advisory Council or in bilateral or multilateral discussions), a further attempt is made to resolve the disagreement immediately before the plenary session is opened. This occurs in the regular, unofficial and non-public, so-called preliminary discussions of the *Bundesrat*, which begin half an hour before the official plenary session. If, however, this informal conference (which takes place in the plenary chamber under the chairmanship of the *Bundesrat* President) does not arrive at a solution, a very peculiar 'institution' comes into play. The Heads of Government of the *Länder* and/or their Plenipotentiaries meet in 'Room 13' of the *Bundesrat* building (adjacent to the plenary chamber) in a final, last-minute attempt to solve crucial problems. In most cases the delay to the start of the plenary session caused by 'Room 13' is the only indication to the public that some complicated knot in the arrangement of *Bundesrat* business has had to be disentangled.

This is not so, of course, in cases in which legislative conflict has arisen between *Bundestag* and *Bundesrat* or between the *Bundesrat* and the Federal Government. On such occasions, the public will be informed officially of the demand by any of these constitutional organs that the Committee of Mediation (*Vermittlungsausschuss*) be convened. Both *Bundestag* and *Bundesrat* have eleven representatives on the Committee of Mediation, the *Bundesrat* nominating one member for each *Land* and the *Bundestag* selecting its eleven members in proportion to party strength. The rules of the Committee are laid down in Article 77, Section 2 of the Basic Law and in the Joint Standing Orders of *Bundestag* and *Bundesrat* on the Committee of Mediation.[14] The Committee meets privately in order to enable it to work out compromises on matters of conflict. Moreover, to make compromise possible the *Bundesrat* members (all of cabinet rank) are not subject to instructions from their *Land* Cabinets or Heads of Government. Furthermore (and in contrast to the Conference Committee of the American Congress), the composition of the Mediation Committee is stabilised by the fact that it is a permanent body for the lifetime of one *Bundestag*, and by the rule that its members and their deputies can only be recalled a maximum of four times within the lifetime of the same *Bundestag*. In order to ensure the passage of the compromise worked out by the Committee, it also has the power to rule in its recommendations that the *Bundestag* can only vote on the whole package of recommendations, and thus cannot reject particular parts of the compromise package. In almost all cases the Committee makes use of this power.

The need to convene the Mediation Committee is very much dependent on the relationship between the party-political majorities in *Bundestag* and *Bundesrat*; conflict is more frequent if different party or coalition majorities exist in each house. If the same party or coalition dominates both houses, the Mediation Committee is convened only infrequently.

In contrast, the permanent Missions of the *Länder* to the Federation are constantly at work. These are headed by the Plenipotentiaries of the *Länder*, who personally spend at least a third of their time in Bonn. The *Länder* civil servants who work in the Missions, however, are permanently resident in Bonn, and commute from there more or less regularly for one or two days per week into their respective *Land* capitals.

In the overall structure of *Bund–Länder* relations the Missions act, in effect, as the 'spiders in the web' for their respective *Länder*, and in this respect they can justifiably be termed as the nucleus of the working relationships between *Bund* and *Länder*. In most cases their civil servants staff the *Bundesrat* committees for their respective *Land*. In addition, the Missions also serve as the overall liaison institutions between *Land* and federal ministries and between each other.[15] This is, of course, particularly the case in *Bundesrat* business. Moreover, the Missions must also, by virtue of the Standing Orders of the Cabinets in both the Federation and the *Länder*, be informed of all other business conducted between any branch of the Federal Government and the executive authorities of their *Länder*.

Furthermore, they report back to their *Land* capitals on all important or otherwise specifically relevant political and committee business in the *Bundestag*. For this purpose their civil servants have the constitutionally guaranteed right of access to all *Bundestag* plenary sessions and committee meetings (Article 43, Section 2 of the Basic Law). The same provision also gives them 'the right to be heard at any time' in the

Bundestag committees, while in plenary sessions this right is in practice exercised by *Länder* ministers or heads of government alone. In the *Bundestag* committees the civil servants of the *Länder* Missions only rarely make use of the right to speak, but they very frequently attend in order to report back as quickly as possible to their *Land* capitals. The reasons for this practice of reporting as soon as possible on the deliberations and results of committee work are to be found in the calendar of legislative procedure, which is enshrined in Article 77, Section 2 of the Basic Law. This stipulates that the right of the *Bundesrat* to demand the convention of the Committee of Mediation in case of a conflict is restricted to a time period of just three weeks, dated from the receipt of the adopted bill from the *Bundestag*. In cases when the *Bundestag* has re-adopted a bill after considering the recommendations of the Mediation Committee, the time-span when the *Bundesrat* is able to raise an objection is just two weeks. These time limits would, in most cases, be far too restrictive for any of the *Länder* governments to make up its mind on its attitude in the *Bundesrat* if the Missions in Bonn could not report immediately on the decisions of *Bundestag* committees.

Besides performing these vital functions within the legislative process, the Missions also serve as constant information sources on important developments in the federal ministries, as well as in the parliamentary party factions. Moreover, in all financial (particularly budgetary) matters and in economic policy developments in Bonn which have relevance for their *Länder*, the Missions have the legitimate and acknowledged task of acting as 'official lobbyists' for their *Länder*.

The Missions also undertake public relations work in Bonn on behalf of their *Länder* (for example by organising cultural and economic exhibitions, lectures, press conferences, concerts, receptions and other social gatherings of various kinds). Similarly, they often organise so-called 'parliamentary evenings' which enable regional or other interest groups, and even individual firms, to discuss their aims and problems with Members of the *Bundestag* and/or representatives of the Federal Government. Within the field of public relations the Missions also receive numerous parties of visitors from the constituencies of *Bundestag* members in their *Land* and give them information on constitutional questions and current issues. The total number of guests of various kinds who visit the Missions is quite considerable.[16]

Last, but not least, the Missions serve as regular meeting places for the groups of *Bundestag* members, within each of the parliamentary party factions, who sit for their respective *Länder*, and assist them in the performance of their functions.

Seen in total, this rather wide-ranging scope of the tasks of the *Länder* Missions in Bonn has, on occasion, led them to be termed the '*Corps Fédéral*' in open allusion to the *Corps Diplomatique* in the federal capital.

The description of the functions of the Missions has already indicated that numerous permanent contacts exist between the civil servants of the Federation and the *Länder*. These are, however, by no means restricted to contacts between the Missions and federal ministries. Alongside these, many meetings are called between civil servants of federal ministries and their equivalents in the *Länder*, either under permanent or *ad hoc* arrangements. The purposes of these meetings are manifold: most of them are held in the process of preparing federal government bills and the drafting of delegated legislation in statutory instruments. The need for the federal ministries to call such meetings is based in the fact that about 50 per cent of all federal legislation (including statutory instruments under Article 80 of the Basic Law) requires the consent of the *Bundesrat*. This again reflects the fact that most federal statutes are administered by the authorities of the *Länder*, with the result that the federal ministries are dependent on their political advice in drafting bills and statutory instruments. In addition, federal statutes may empower ministries or other authorities of the *Länder* to issue ordinances, under their own responsibility, to facilitate the execution of federal statutes. Other reasons for the calling of meetings between federal and *Länder* civil servants may arise from the process of allocating federal funds or by a whole range of other matters of joint relevance.

Conferences of Federal Ministers and their counterparts in the *Länder* are very often prepared by such contacts. In some fields these conferences have an institutional and regular character. In others, they are convened on an *ad hoc* basis for some special reason (but nonetheless fairly frequently).

Besides this day-to-day cooperation in federal matters in various bodies and conferences, there are also the special institutions of 'cooperative federalism'. The most prominent among these are the Financial Planning Commission (*Finanzplanungsrat*) and the Planning Commissions for Joint Tasks.[17]

The 'Third Level'

The final level of coordination is that of horizontal cooperation among the *Länder* themselves (the 'Third Level'). The highest ranking of the institutions in this field is the Conference of Minister-Presidents (Heads of Government of the *Länder*), which meets formally once a year, but which convenes in practice more regularly – at least once before conferences with the Chancellor, and quite often more frequently than that. The chairmanship in these meetings alternates between the *Länder*, and all of them are prepared by meetings of the Heads of the *Länder* Cabinet Offices (*Chefs der Staats- und Senatskanzleien*).

One step below this level there are the conferences of equivalent ministries from different *Länder* whose responsibilities cover the same area of policy (for example housing, education and so on). These are staffed and prepared partly by the *Bundesrat* committee secretariats, and partly (as, for example, in the case of the Conference of Ministers of Housing) by organisational units of their own which may be attached to one of the Missions of the *Länder* in Bonn.

In addition, there are numerous formal and informal contacts between the civil servants of equivalent ministries in different *Länder*, which exclude their federal counterparts. Their purpose is either to prepare meetings on the federal level, or to coordinate among themselves specific actions or legislation in either the federal or the *Länder* sphere.

Political coordination between the three levels

All institutions on all three levels (*Gesamtstaat*, *Bundesstaat* and 'Third Level') are interlinked by a network of bilateral or multilateral contacts and, in some fields, by further bodies and institutions with a party-political orientation which are activated if and when issues of potential party-political controversy arise. These serve both as 'alarm systems' and as coordinating machineries, particularly in the relationship between the federal structure and the parliamentary party factions in the *Bundestag*. Some of them (especially the Conferences of Party Leaders in the *Bundestag* and the *Land* Legislatures and the Executive Committees of the parties on the federal level) have been depicted already. Others include the regular meetings of the Plenipotentiaries of those *Länder* in which the majority party or coalition is either politically aligned with or opposed to the Federal Government. The timing of these is coordinated with the calendar of *Bundesrat* plenary sessions.[18] There are also *ad hoc* conferences of representatives of politically aligned *Länder* which precede crucial *Bundesrat* committee meetings, and which take place either on political or civil service level.[19] Similar conferences can also precede any of the other institutional contacts already discussed if the political need arises. This is regularly the case before the Conferences of the Federal Chancellor with the Heads of *Länder* Governments, the meetings of the Mediation Committee and the Conferences of the Minister-Presidents and the Heads of their Cabinet Offices.

Very discreetly organised contacts also take place whenever the need arises for the *Bundesrat* to elect one of the sixteen justices of the Federal Constitutional Court. According to Article 94, Section 1 of the Basic Law, half of the justices are to 'be elected by the *Bundestag* and half by the *Bundesrat*'. While the *Bundestag* has delegated this power to a special

Committee for the Selection of Justices (*Richterwahlausschuss*), the *Bundesrat* elects its justices in plenary session. However, informal political contacts concerning the selection process do, of course, precede the plenary session. For some time now, the custom has developed that the Minister-Presidents of North-Rhine-Westphalia (on behalf of the SPD-governed *Länder*, or so-called '*A-Länder*') and Rhineland-Palatinate (on behalf of the *Länder* governed by the CDU or CSU, or by CDU-led coalitions, the so-called '*B-Länder*') coordinate the contacts between each other and with their respective parliamentary parties in the *Bundestag*.

Evaluation of the working structure of German federalism

Returning briefly to the opening remarks of this chapter, it is hoped that after the above attempt to explain the working structure of German federalism, the German system no longer appears to be so 'odd' – though it certainly must be admitted that it is a complicated network! However, this is always – and inevitably – both the trademark and the price of any federal system. It is the price to be paid for the addition of a vertical dimension of the separation of powers to the horizontal one between the legislative, executive and judicial branches of government. The broad political and popular acceptance of the federal system indicates that this price is felt to be well paid. It is also certain – again returning to the opening remarks of the chapter – that the system 'works', at least in terms of executive efficiency. Less certain, however, is whether or not the 'system as it stands' provides for an adequate constitutional relationship between *Bund* and *Länder*, and, in particular, whether or not it fulfils democratic requirements. These considerations are the subject of this section.

Germany's concept of federalism is not that of the 'dual state' as embodied in the philosophy (though perhaps not the practice) of American federalism. It does not consist of two separate structures, each fully equipped, institutionally and administratively, in its own field of competence. Instead, it represents an interwoven system characterised above all by the fact that the *Länder* both execute federal legislation and participate in its creation under a clearly defined responsibility of their own (as in Articles 30, 50 and 88 of the Basic Law).

In addition, it should be emphasised that there have always been substantial elements of 'cooperative federalism' in the German system – even before the constitutional reforms of 1966–9 (the introduction of Joint Tasks) – which will certainly be maintained in the future. The German system has never been one of discrete units existing beside or below one another, with clear-cut and separate catalogues of competences. The attempts at instituting such a system – more or less imposed on the original federal constitution at the behest of the occupying powers in 1949 – only led to the so-called 'grey zones' of federal financing which developed in the years from 1949 to 1966. The concept of cooperative federalism recommended by the Troeger Commission in 1966,[20] which led to the constitutional reforms of the Grand Coalition between 1966 and 1969 was, therefore, nothing but a logical consequence of the practical needs for close cooperation between *Bund* and *Länder*. These needs had been neglected in constitutional terms in the early years of the Federal Republic not so much because of the views of the framers of the Basic Law, but because of the influence of the occupying powers (predominantly the French) in their clearly understandable post-war desire to prevent a revival of German nationalism by decentralising political power.

Nevertheless, there has always been a strong doctrine within the Basic Law that *Bund* and *Länder* have a 'separate but equal' relationship. Although this phrase is admittedly taken from quite a different context,[21] it can be used here as a means of illustrating the defects and pointing out the criticisms of the 'system as it stands'. This constitutional doctrine – and the problems it incorporates – is reflected in two main areas. The first is the requirement in Article 29, Section 1 of the Basic Law 'that the *Länder* by their size and capacity are able effectively to fulfil the functions incumbent on them' in both the political and the economic spheres. The second 'problem area' is contained in Article 106, Section 3.2 of the Basic Law, which requires the whole system to guarantee equality in the conditions of life in the whole federal territory in order to ensure a 'uniformity of living standards'. Doubts about the ability of all of the *Länder* – whose size and resources vary greatly – to fulfil their political and economic functions adequately and to ensure a uniformity of living standards have led to pressure for reform. Accordingly, during Willy Brandt's Chancellorship in the early 1970s, reform commissions were set up to look at both of these problem areas: the Federal Government Commission on the Reorganisation of the Federal Territory, the so-called Ernst Commission, which sat from 1970 to 1972 and reported to the Chancellor in 1973,[22] and the Parliamentary Commission of Inquiry on Constitutional Reform, which was set up in 1970, reconvened after the general elections in 1972, and which reported to the *Bundestag* in 1976.[23]

These commissions submitted far-reaching recommendations with regard to decreasing the number of the *Länder* and to introducing a federal system of planning which would enable the federation to guarantee equality of living conditions. However, due to a combination of adverse political circumstances, none of these recommendations could be implemented.[24]

The problems which motivated the recommendations for reform in the 1970s therefore still await resolution. In particular, the working relationships between the executive branches of *Bund* and *Länder* are too complex and too dense in some areas. This limits the transparency of *Bund–Länder* relations as far as the general public is concerned and tends to undermine the autonomy and responsibility of the *Land* legislatures. It is also evident that the dense network of *Bund–Länder* relations allows the federation to interfere in many areas which are constitutionally the domain of the *Länder* by the mere impact of its financial 'golden lead'. In the field of co-financing in particular, the *Bund* feels invited, and in many instances even compelled to intervene in view of the fact that some of the *Länder* are financially not in a position to offer their full share in the task of guaranteeing uniform living standards. Some critics of the system have gone so far as to say in this respect that the step has been taken from a cooperative to a 'corruptive' federalism!

Even if we ignore this rather provocative formulation of the problem, the fact remains that the present shape of German federalism has led to the paradox where the constitutional requirement of guaranteeing uniform living standards is countered by the fact that the performance of the individual *Länder* in achieving this goal is uneven. The reason for this paradox clearly lies in the preservation of a *Länder* community whose members are unequally equipped, in terms of territorial, financial and administrative capacity, to fulfil that goal. The inequalities in the performance of the *Länder* in carrying out their constitutional tasks and, more generally, the relatively large number of *Länder* contained within a relatively small territory would seem to call for a reduction in their number combined with an improvement in the balance between them both individually, as compared with each other, and collectively between them and the *Bund*.

Reforms in this field would enhance the political vitality and economic productivity of the system as a whole. It would also slim the necessary machinery of *Bund–Länder* relations and would thus make the system more transparent and leave more room for autonomous and responsible parliamentary decision-making in the *Länder*. It would also be necessary to accompany such reforms by modifying existing financial and planning arrangements. Such steps could enhance the potential for achieving interregional financial equilibrium and for taking into account the need to compensate for the special demands and needs of individual *Länder*. They could also improve the practice of joint planning both by developing a more transparent system and by institutionalising the exchange of political innovation, as is, for example, practised by the American states in a system of regular information exchange on solutions found for newly identified political, social or economic problems.[25]

While steps of this kind and scope are unlikely in the near future, they are bound to stay on the agenda. Even the failure of the reform initiatives of the 1970s[26] and the dilution of Article 29 of the Basic Law in 1976 (when the original obligation of the *Bund* to reform the size and number of the *Länder*, if the need arose, was changed into a mere option to do so) have not abolished the underlying *ratio legis* of the constitutional demand for uniformity. This would seem to be underlined by the various (but up to now rather ineffective) attempts at coordination between the city-states of Hamburg and Bremen and their neighbouring *Länder*, Schleswig-Holstein and Lower Saxony, in the north of the Federal Republic. These parts of the federation in particular will hardly survive in the long run in their present organisational form without some kind of federal territorial reform.

Other aspects of previous reform plans have been more or less abandoned. These would include the idea of substantially realigning the distribution of legislative powers between *Bund* and *Länder*, the introduction of a comprehensive system of constitutionally fixed joint planning between *Bund* and *Länder*, a fundamental dilution of the concept of cooperative federalism and a 'semi-parliamentarisation' of the *Bundesrat* (by incorporating within it members chosen by the *Land* legislatures on the basis of party representation). A comprehensive system of joint planning was rejected in the final report of the Parliamentary Commission of Inquiry on Constitutional Reform in 1976[27] in favour of a more limited system restricted to particularly important needs and projects (although the same commission had previously recommended a comprehensive system in its interim report in 1972).[28] The Parliamentary Commission also rejected plans to reconstruct the *Bundesrat* by incorporating representatives of the oppositions in the *Land* legislatures on the basis that this would too drastically change both the constitutional position and the political and administrative working methods of the second chamber.[29]

Potential reforms of the working structure of German federalism on these lines have therefore lost much of their impetus, while territorial reforms seem to have fallen to the bottom of the agenda. However, criticism of a further problem, the frequency and scale of party-political influence within the German federal structure, still remains strong. Such criticism focuses on the notion that legitimate regional interests, constitutional institutions (such as the Mediation Committee) and the role of administrative experience in the legislative process tend to be deformed or eroded by the sometimes misplaced use of party pressure.

During the period of the Social–Liberal coalition from 1969 to 1982, when the SPD–FDP majority in the *Bundestag* was countered by a *Bundesrat* dominated throughout the entire time-span by CDU/CSU-led *Länder*, this was a highly controversial and much debated matter. The political and constitutional discussion focused around the fact that the conservative majority in the *Bundesrat* very frequently (and, in the eyes of many observers, excessively) called upon the powers of the Committee of Mediation to alter or even block decisions of the *Bundestag*. During this period, the Mediation Committee was convened at the request of the *Bundesrat* 213 times and the consent of the *Bundesrat* to federal bills was withheld some forty-three times. The picture has changed substantially since 1982, when the CDU/CSU, in coalition with the FDP, regained the majority in both houses. Since then, the *Bundesrat* has only demanded the convention of the Mediation Committee on six occasions, and none of these resulted in a refusal to consent to federal bills.[30]

Nonetheless, there have, of course, been vital conflicts between federal and regional interests since 1982, such as, for instance, those arising from the various financial implications the Tax Reform Act of 1990 has had for the *Länder*. However, these conflicts are now no longer resolved in the Committee of Mediation (although this is the institution created by the Basic Law for this purpose). Instead, the practice has been developed of 'coordinating them away behind closed doors' in special and non-public meetings of the CDU/CSU *Länder* with top-level representatives of the Federal Government (see Hartmut Klatt's chapter in this volume). This has resulted in a certain erosion in public awareness of the needs of federalism as distinct from those of the political parties.

While the controversies during the period 1969–82 centred around the accusation that the *Bundesrat* was being abused for the purposes of opposition in the *Bundestag*, complaints now focus upon the lack of consultation with the SPD-led *Länder* and, consequently, the perceived political and financial injustice being done to them. Such complaints have been particularly numerous and strong since the combined effects of the Tax Reform Act of 1990, and the need for a basic reconstruction of the financial arrangements between *Bund* and *Länder* (stemming from a judgment of the Federal Constitutional Court), led to the passage of an Act on Structural Aid for the economically weaker parts of the *Länder* community.

Challenge and opportunity: unification of Europe

Under the growing impact of the approaching Single Market in the European Community, and with the transfer of new powers to the Community under the terms of the Single European Act, the European dimension has had a significant influence on the working structures of German federalism. The European dimension has been an important factor ever since Article 2 of the Act of Ratification of the Treaty of

Rome in 1957 gave the right of comment and recommendation on draft European legislation to both *Bundesrat* and *Bundestag*.[31] The Single European Act and the approach of the Single Market has resulted (and will continue to result), however, in further substantial increases in the weight of the European factor which, potentially at least, could signal a redistribution of power away from the *Länder* and into the hands of the *Bund*.

Progress in European integration need not, however, necessarily mean a threat to German federalism. But it does require the building up of new forms of institutional relationship between *Bund* and *Länder*, and also between the organs of the Community and the federal state. Such forms of relationship have existed – and are still in the process of being further developed – ever since the *Bundesrat* and the *Länder* successfully strengthened their influence in European affairs within the framework of the West German constitutional system in 1986, when, after a long struggle with the Federal Government, a stronger institutional position was established for the *Bundesrat* and the *Länder* under Article 2 of the Act of Ratification of the Single European Act.[32] The institutional and procedural innovations initiated by these new rules are addressed in detail elsewhere in this volume, and will not, therefore, be discussed further here.[33] Such innovations may ultimately be embodied in the constitution itself. The *Bundesrat* has recently initiated a Bill to this effect which would, if successful, amend Article 24 of the Basic Law, in particular with a view to anchoring constitutionally the need to secure the *Bundesrat*'s consent to transfers of sovereign rights to the European Community.[34]

While these changes – actual and potential – remain firmly within the framework of the German constitution, a new dimension of federal relevance has begun to develop on the level of the European Community itself. This concentrates on the notion of a 'Europe of the Regions'. With its Resolution on Regional Policy in the Community and the Role of the Regions of 18 November 1988, and with the Draft of a Community Charter on Regionalisation embodied within it,[35] the European Parliament has attempted to give this concept rather more substance. Meanwhile, the *Bundesrat* has passed a Resolution which by and large supports the suggestions of the European Parliament.[36] Following this, Bavaria tabled a Draft Resolution in the *Bundesrat* on 13 March 1990 concerning the participation of the *Länder* in the EC Member Governments' Conference on Amending the Community Treaties. In this draft resolution the demand is raised by the 'setting out of rights of *participation of* Länder *and Regions in the process of decision-making on the European level*'. The resolution further charges the *Bundesrat* with the presentation of 'concrete suggestions' to this effect.[37] The *Bundesrat* will probably pass a Resolution on these lines in its plenary session on 6 April 1990. Moreover, the matter will certainly remain subject to further discussion in the Conference of Minister Presidents.[38]

However, any deliberations on this matter have to take into account the fact that the idea of a 'Europe of the Regions' remains, for the time being, a rather dim concept which needs to be properly clarified. Nevertheless, such a concept does hold out some prospect of reducing the 'democratic deficit' of the European Community, as well as its tendencies towards overcentralisation. Particularly in the light of such tendencies, this concept should not be allowed to become a tool to weaken rather than strengthen the regions of Europe. The negligible powers accorded by the EC Commission to its Advisory Council of Regional and Local Government Bodies could be a hint that this may, indeed, be the case.

If, however, a properly balanced concept of a 'Europe of the Regions' is developed, its implementation would certainly require profound changes both in the territorial and in the functional structures of German federalism, together with its internal working relationships. Whether or not this would ultimately usher in a return to 'the old nations of Europe', with a progressive dissolution of the present member states of the EC remains a matter of conjecture. However, any regionalising reform which would result in the cutting away and destruction of such a network of working relationships, as has been described in this chapter, would be fraught with problems. It would be a task similar to that of Shakespeare's Shylock in *The Merchant of Venice*: to cut out a pound of flesh without losing a drop of blood. It would be both impossible and fatal.

Moreover, the European Community is facing enormous new challenges under the impact of the developments currently taking place in East Central and Eastern Europe. The ability of the EC to cope with these challenges and to respond to the demands placed on it by the states in these regions would tend to suggest that it will concentrate on the preservation and strengthening of its own and its member states' existing working structures, rather than embarking on any fundamental structural reforms. The present priorities of the EC are to complete the Single Market and to take steps to open its structures to the states of East Central and Eastern Europe. Already, Hungary has formally notified her interest in (eventual) full EC membership, and others are likely to follow. In addition, the completion of the Single Market will have to be followed by negotiations on new applications for EC membership from EFTA states (of which Austria has already formally tabled her application). In face of these very substantial problems and challenges, it is hard to imagine that the EC would simultaneously initiate fundamental changes in its existing structure such as a profound shift of constitutional powers from the member states to their regions or a 'Europeanisation' of the regions would imply. This point applies all the more if one takes into account the present heterogeneity of the regions throughout the EC, both in terms of constitutional status and of political cohesion within their own national environments.

It would appear, then, that a genuine regionalisation of Europe – together with the fundamental effects on the working relationships between *Bund* and *Länder* which would ensue – is inconceivable for the next decade at least. This does not, however, rule out the idea of regionalisation for all time. As noted above, regionalisation could become not just a tool, but also a necessity in protecting against overcentralisation within EC institutions after further transfers of sovereign rights from present and future member states.[39] The nucleus of the concept of regionalisation – the awareness that the nations of twentieth-century Europe need not necessarily be identical with the component parts of the EC of the twenty-first century – will therefore retain its relevance.

Notes

1. This is a revised version of a paper presented at the Conference 'Forty years of West German federalism' at the Centre for Federal Studies, Leicester University, in September 1989. Some of the themes in the chapter are developed further by the author in Chapter 9 of this volume, which takes account of the potential impact of recent events in German politics on the future structures of German federalism.
2. For work in English on this topic, see Nevil Johnson, *Federalism and decentralisation in the Federal Republic of Germany*, Research Paper No. 1 of the Commission on the Constitution, HMSO, London (1973), 30–8; Advisory Commission on Intergovernmental Relations, *Studies in comparative federalism: Australia, Canada, the United States and West Germany*, Washington, DC (1981). For a recent evaluation in German, see Wolfgang Renzsch, 'Föderale Finanzbeziehungen im Bundesstaat', *Zeitschrift für Parlamentsfragen*, (1989), 331–44.
3. For the text of this and all other articles of the Basic Law quoted in this chapter, see the Appendix to this volume.
4. As in Article 91a of the Basic Law, concerning higher education institutions, the improvement of regional economic structures, of agricultural structure and of coastal preservation.
5. As in Article 91b of the Basic Law, concerning educational planning and the promotion of scientific research of supraregional importance. For federal investment aids in other relevant fields of *Länder* competence, see Article 104a of the Basic Law, as reproduced in the Appendix of this volume.
6. See *Handbuch des Bundesrats 1989/90*, 101ff.
7. According to this rule, it is the purpose of these conferences 'to discuss important political, social and financial questions and to contribute to a

mutually understood, uniform course of politics in the Federation and the *Länder* by maintaining personal contacts' between the Chancellor and the Heads of the *Länder* Governments.

8. The formal 'Agreement on the Renewal of the Joint Parliamentary Group of CDU and CSU for the 11th *Bundestag*' of 16 February 1987 states in section 9: 'The CDU/CSU Parliamentary Group will make no amendments to the Basic Law which the CSU opposes for reasons of upholding the principles of the federal state order. The same applies to legislative projects in the field of the European Community which impinge upon the constitutional competences of the *Länder* or on their essential interests.' This Agreement has had corresponding predecessors at the beginning of each new *Bundestag*.

9. Plenary business consists of federal legislation (including any statutory instruments arising from it, if they require the consent of the *Bundesrat*), the reviewing and passing of statements on draft European secondary legislation, general administrative rules which facilitate the execution of federal statutes, any *Bundesrat* resolutions tabled on the above-mentioned areas of business, elections of *Bundesrat* or *Länder* representatives to Federal Administrative Boards, election of justices to the Federal Constitutional Court, and – rather more rarely – comments of the *Bundesrat* on law suits pending in this Court.

10. From 1949 to 1987 there were 5,068 committee meetings and 2,667 sub-committee sessions. See *Handbuch des Bundesrats 1989/90*, 239.

11. In 1989–90 the chairmanships were distributed as follows: Agriculture – Rhineland-Palatinate; Employment and Social Affairs – Hesse; Foreign Affairs – North-Rhine-Westphalia; European Community Matters – Baden-Württemberg; Finance – North-Rhine-Westphalia; Inner-German Relations – Baden Württemberg; Home Affairs – Schleswig-Holstein; Youth, Family and Health – Saarland; Cultural Affairs – Berlin; Legal Affairs – Hamburg; Environment, Nature Conservation and Nuclear Reactor Safety – Lower Saxony; Transport and Postal Services – Bremen; Defence – Bavaria; Economy – Bavaria. The chairmanship of the so-called 'political committees (Foreign Affairs, Inner-German Relations and Defence) rotates annually. All others are held permanently, although they are subject to a formal annual re-election process.

12. Discussions on *Bundesrat* plenary business are regularly held in preparation for the Advisory Council's work by an informal, but indispensable conference bringing together the civil servants who coordinate *Bundesrat* business in the Missions of the *Länder* and the secretaries of the *Bundesrat* committees.

13. No. 9 of the *Bundesrat* Standing Orders. For further details, see *Handbuch des Bundesrats 1989/90*, 105.

14. *Handbuch des Bundesrats 1989/90*, 147–9.

15. The heads of civil service staff in the Missions meet regularly, and all of the Missions' civil servants are in regular business, political and social contact with one another.

16. For instance, the Lower Saxon Mission receives an average of approximately 25,000 guests per annum. Including visitors to exhibitions, there

have been approximately one million guests in the Mission since it was established in 1949–50.

17. See notes 4 and 5.

18. Once again, these political meetings are prepared by the heads of the civil service staff in the Missions concerned and/or by the civil servants responsible for *Bundesrat* coordination within the Missions.

19. In most cases civil servants of the Missions also participate in the meetings of the various policy committees of the parliamentary parties which precede *Bundestag* committee sessions.

20. Named after its chairman. See Kommission für die Finanzreform, *Gutachten über die Finanzreform in der Bundesrepublik Deutschland*, Stuttgart (1986).

21. i.e. one of the phases in the jurisdiction of the US Supreme Court concerning racial discrimination.

22. Sachverständigenkommission für die Neugliederung des Bundesgebiets, *Vorschläge zur Neugliederung des Bundesgebiets gemäss Art. 29 des Grundgesetzes*, Bonn (1972). The author of this chapter served as the liaison officer of the Federal Chancellor's Office in this Commission.

23. *Bundestags-Drucksache 7/5924*, reprinted in Presse- und Informations-zentrum des Deutschen Bundestages (ed.), *Zur Sache: Beratungen und Empfehlungen zur Verfassungsreform. Teil 1: Parlament und Regierung*, Bonn (1976); *Teil 2: Bund und Länder*, Bonn (1977). The Federal Chancellor's Office followed the deliberations of this Commission through its Planning Division, in which the author was employed from 1971 to 1973.

24. See Alfred Kubel, 'Bewährungen und Versäumnisse im Bundesstaat', in Rudolf Hrbek (ed.), *Miterlebt – Mitgestaltet. Der Bundesrat im Rückblick*, Bonn Aktuell, Stuttgart (1989), 50–64.

25. See, for example, the annual publications on *Suggested State Legislation*, issued by the American Council of State Governments in Lexington, Kentucky.

26. See Uwe Leonardy, 'Halten wir den Staat für perfekt?', *Die Neue Gesellschaft* (1978), 194–9.

27. See note 23.

28. *Bundestags-Drucksache 6/3829*, reported in Presse- und Informationsamt der Bundesregierung (ed.), *Zur Sache: Fragen der Verfassungsreform. Zwischen-bericht der Enquete-Kommission des deutschen Bundestages – Parlamentsreform, Internationale Probleme, Planung und Gesetzgebung*, Bonn (1973).

29. See note 23.

30. *Handbuch des Bundesrats 1989/90*, 242–3.

31. For a comparison of the use of this right by the two houses, see Uwe Leonardy, 'Bundestag und Europäische Gemeinschaft: Notwendigkeit und Umfeld eines Europa-Ausschusses', *Zeitschrift für Parlamentsfragen*, (1989), 527–44.

32. This was followed by a *Bund–Länder* Agreement Concerning European Community Matters of 17 December 1937. See *Handbuch des Bundesrats 1989/90*, 15–60. On the development of the constitutional position of the *Bundesrat* in EC matters, see Sekretariat des Bundesrats (ed.), *Bundesrat und Europäische Gemeinschaften*, Bonn (1988).

33. See Rudolf Hrbek's contribution to this volume. It should be emphasised here, however, that these rules were introduced not only for reasons of distributing legislative power, but also equally due to the fact that the execution of European secondary legislation is, in most fields, also a task of the *Länder* and not of the Federation.

34. *Bundesrats-Drucksache 703/89 (Beschluss)*, 16 March 1990.

35. *Official Gazette of the EC (German Edition)*, No. C 326, 19 December 1988, 289.

36. *Bundesrats-Drucksache 279/89 (Beschluss)*, 16 February 1990.

37. *Bundesrats-Drucksache 198/90 (Neu)*, 13 March 1990.

38. Furthermore, this matter is also on the agenda of the Conference of Presidents of European Parliamentary Assemblies in Brussels on 8–9 June 1990, where the President of the *Bundesrat*, Governing Mayor Walter Momper of Berlin, will present a report.

39. Björn Engholm, Minister President of Schleswig Holstein and President of the *Bundesrat* in 1988–9, sees 'a flowering of the regional idea to the same extent as the member states give up powers in favour of European unity'. See *Sozialdemokratischer Pressedienst EUROPA*, 7 December 1989, 9.

4 Federalism, legalism and political reality: the record of the Federal Constitutional Court[1]

Philip Blair

Federalism ... means legalism – the predominance of the judiciary in the constitution – the prevalence of a spirit of legality among the people. (Dicey, *Law of the Constitution*)

Constitutional disputes are always political disputes: therein lies the problematical nature of the whole institution. (Triepel)

If taken together, the above quotations, however different the standpoint of their authors, sum up the problems of adjudication of disputes between the different levels of government within a federal system.

The justification for Dicey's dictum derives, of course, from the fact that a genuine federal relationship, such as is to be found in West Germany, presupposes the subordination of both the federal authorities and the member States to a constitution which apportions the powers of government between them and which neither level can alter unilaterally.

Such an arrangement entails the need for an independent arbiter of disputes which inevitably arise as to observance of the dividing-line between the powers of each level and of their mutual rights and duties; and since these practical issues affecting the political room for manoeuvre of each level of government have been made questions of constitutional law, the task of providing an authoritative settlement of them is normally entrusted to a court. In the case of West Germany, this is the *Bundesverfassungsgericht*.

Whether such consequences of the common subjection to an overriding legal framework are sufficient to justify Dicey's charge of legalism and the predominance of the judiciary may, however, be doubted. It is certainly true that political life in Germany takes place to a striking degree within, and with reference to, a legal framework. The tendency still persists to aim at comprehensive regulation by legal norms, to assert constitutional–legal justification for political actions and demands, and to seek authoritative, definitive and hence legally binding resolution of conflict. But this disposition, like the notorious *'Juristenmonopol'* which both results from and perpetuates it, is explicable rather in terms of certain peculiar historical circumstances in Germany than by reference to the federal structure. However, that is not to deny that the political authorities, already hedged around with a wide range of relatively detailed constitutional constraints, find themselves subject, by virtue of the federal system, to a further dimension of checks and balances: in this respect, the 'guardian of the constitution' is strategically placed to exercise influence on the distribution of power within the political system.

The jurisdiction of the Federal Constitutional Court

The role of the Constitutional Court in the federal system is necessarily affected by a number of factors. The most obvious of these is the range of its jurisdiction. Here it should be borne in mind that the *Bundesverfassungsgericht* is not a general court of final appeal like the US Supreme Court but may only determine constitutional questions. However, it has comprehensive jurisdiction for all questions of Federal constitutional law, and access to it is easier than in most federal systems. Its competence to decide disputes as to the rights and duties of the Federation and the member States by means of an adversarial process known as a *'Verfassungsstreit'* may be close to practice in other countries. But the so-called abstract review of norms (*'abstrakte Normenkontrolle'*) – the determination of whether a norm of Federal or *Land* law is in conformity with the Basic Law, or whether *Land* law conforms with other Federal law – can be directly initiated by the Federal or a *Land* government or by one-third of the members of the *Bundestag* without reference to a concrete case affecting them directly.

This procedure has no direct parallel in the English-speaking world. It makes it considerably easier for one or more governments to seek a judicial ruling on a legislative provision to which they object, whether or not the issue is a federal one. In 1962, Konrad Hesse, later to become a Constitutional Court judge, asserted in his book *Der unitarische Bundesstaat*: 'Disputes between *Bund* and *Länder* are today, as is well known, as a rule no longer true federal disputes but disputes between political alignments within the federal state, which are cast in the guise of federal disputes and settled by recourse to constitutional litigation.'[2] The abstract judicial review procedure does indeed encourage litigation by actors in the federal system to frustrate political projects of their opponents at another level. Moreover, such cases are undoubtedly those which have produced the greatest éclat. Federal disputes with party-political implications include the Concordat Case, the case concerning local referendums on arming the *Bundeswehr* with tactical nuclear weapons, and the famous Television Case, all of which are referred to below, as well as two major cases concerning the *Bundesrat's* right of veto over controversial legislation. A number of 'quasi-federal' cases may also be identified where, although the dispute is between *Länder* and the Federal Government, the issue is not even ostensibly about powers or duties in the federal system, but about party finance, the validity of the Basic Treaty with the German Democratic Republic, or the reform of abortion law and the right to life. In reality they are cases of *Länder* governments of the same political colour as the Federal Opposition acting on behalf of, or in alliance with, the latter.

In fact, however, what is remarkable is how few such cases there have been. Of federal disputes with party-political implications there have been seven or eight, while there have been no more than a handful of 'quasi-federal' disputes. At the same time, there have been some two dozen 'pure' federal disputes, where party-political considerations were marginal or absent. These include many relatively undramatic cases concerning, for example, the law on public officials and their emoluments. But some cases which have attracted much more public attention must also be classed in this category, such as the remarkable one in 1986 arising from applications by no less than six *Länder* governments against various provisions of the Federal law organising the system of financial equalisation between the *Länder* (see below).

In purely numerical terms, however, the most prolific sources of federal cases before the Constitutional Court is the so-called concrete judicial review: when another court, in the context of a specific case before it, considers a relevant provision of Federal or *Land* law to be unconstitutional, it must refer the constitutional issue to the *Bundesverfassungsgericht*. The cases which reach Karlsruhe by this means are seldom so dramatic as those raised by the Federal or *Länder* governments themselves; but they provide numerous opportunities to refine the demarcation of the powers of the two levels of government and, in comparatively uncontroversial circumstances, to establish guidelines for future development.

The context of judicial decision-making

While Dicey warns against the extent to which federal systems place decisions on political matters in the hands of judges, the remark by Triepel is that of a lawyer who accepted that the high court of state must pass judgment on political disputes when they were cast in constitutional terms; there might, however, be consequences for how the judges went about their work. The reaction of the West German Constitutional Court to the political context of its decision-making is the subject of the rest of this chapter. Here it will suffice to allude in advance to three background conditions which bear on the relationship of the Karlsruhe judges with their political environment and, in effect, which make their task easier.

The first concerns the system of appointment to the Court. Half of the judges are selected by a special electoral committee of the *Bundestag*, the other half by the *Bundesrat*, and thus to that extent by the governments of the Länder. With one or two notable (especially Bavarian) exceptions, it cannot be demonstrated that this has greatly affected the attitude of the judges to federal matters, since other criteria have predominated. But it has at least ensured that they are not unduly dependent on the Federal authorities and that the composition of the Court – unlike that of its American counterpart – has never become a serious problem.

The second background condition is the character of the West German federal system. By comparison even with quite recent periods of German history, the *Länder* of the Federal Republic, for reasons which are well known, cannot be said to represent territorial communities marked by sharply distinct cultural identities, let alone ethnic antagonisms or separatist aspirations. This means that the federal issues which come before the Constitutional Court, in contrast to what has sometimes been the case elsewhere, do not spring from conflicts on which the federal structure has been superimposed; rather, they are the result of the friction cases by the institution of the federal system itself. Such issues are much more amenable to judicial resolution.

Thirdly, a comparison with other federal constitutions, especially in the English-speaking world, shows that the Basic Law of the Federal Republic is, on the one hand, relatively detailed and precise and, on the other hand, relatively easy to amend. These characteristics have consequences for the ability of, and the need for, the Constitutional Court to play a creative role in adapting the constitution to changed circumstances.

Having thus set the scene, it remains to examine the influence of the Court over the development of federal relations in practice, and in particular to show that the second and third background conditions just mentioned have not restricted the importance of the Court's role as much as might be expected.

Broad construction and implied power

Given the nature of the division of legislative powers between the Federation and the *Länder*, whereby the former has competence to legislate only on those matters which are specified in the Basic Law and the residual competence belongs to the *Länder*, probably the most important question in relation to the rulings of the Constitutional Court is how far it has been willing to countenance a generous interpretation of these powers. Its significance is increased by the fact that by comparison with some other federal systems the enumeration of Federal legislative powers in Articles 73 and especially 74 is so lengthy that to construe them broadly would be to risk reducing the *Länder* to little more than administrative authorities.

It may indeed be for this reason that the decisions of the Constitutional Court have fairly consistently stressed the presumption in favour of the *Länder* enunciated in Article 30 of the Basic Law and restated with respect to legislative competence in Article 70 and the execution of Federal laws in Article 83. The consequent need to interpret the catalogue of Federal powers strictly has constantly been reiterated by the Court. However, that does not mean that it has always followed it in specific cases. Thus in the early Building Law Opinion[3] it did not hesitate to interpret *Land* law (as in Article 74, No. 18 of the Basic Law) as embracing planning law. Moreover, the major field of economic matters (Article 74, No. 11) has on several occasions been interpreted extensively. For example, in the early Investment Assistance Case[4], the First Senate ruled that the legislative power of the Federation was not limited to those aspects of the economy specifically enumerated in the relevant paragraph. Again, in a much later decision[5], the Second Senate reiterated an earlier finding that 'trade', as part of a law relating to economic matters, was to be interpreted 'comprehensively'; it then cited constitutional precedents from before 1933 to justify a ruling whereby the technical safety of installations used not in the exercise of a trade but nevertheless in undertakings with an economic purpose (in this case lifts in rented blocks of flats) fell under the Federal economic power rather than the *Länder* responsibility for public safety and order.

Such an approach, which is reminiscent of the use made by the US Supreme Court of the 'inter-state commerce' clause, could seriously erode the powers of the *Länder*. But it is the exception. Even the economic power sometimes receives a far from generous interpretation, as is shown, for example, by a judgment, concerning an interest-free, repayable levy on higher salaries which the new Federal Government introduced in 1982.[6] This levy had the stated purpose of financing additional subventions for housing construction and the general aim of stimulating the economy. The Karlsruhe judges refused to accept that it was covered either by the Federal competence for economic matters or by that for housing (though, admittedly, the Court's primary concern was to avert the danger that such repayable levies might be a means of circumventing and undermining the clear apportionment of fiscal powers in the financial section of the Basic Law).

Given that an uncompromising application of the principle of Article 30 of the Basis Law is the norm, it is only logical that the Constitutional Court has been cautious in its use of those instruments of constitutional exegesis which have been favoured by Supreme Courts of English-speaking federations as a means of extensive interpretation, in particular the doctrine of implied powers. Indeed, the derivation of Federal legislative competence from a material connection ('*Sachzusammenhang*') with explicitly assigned powers is on the whole played down by comparison with judicial practice under the Empire or the Weimar Republic, which assumed that the *Reich* had all powers necessary for the full and effective exercise of explicitly granted powers. The possibility is often considered, only to be rejected in most cases; or else it is reasoned that the connection with a particular Federal competence will have to be stronger than that with a recognised power of the *Länder*: in this way the concept of incidental powers becomes a two-edged weapon and the *Länder* can occasionally be the beneficiaries.[7]

In the light of its jurisprudence in some other fields, there is no reason to suppose that the Court's reticence derives merely from a narrow, positivist approach. Rather, the desire to maintain a balance in a federal system whose apportionment of powers was already loaded in the Federal Government's favour can be assumed to have played a part. A brief look will now be taken at a number of aspects of federal adjudication which might be expected to give the Court an opportunity to reinforce the position of the *Länder*.

The 'need' for Federal legislation in the concurrent sphere

The bulk of legislative powers in the Federal Republic belong to the concurrent category. Particular importance therefore attaches to the application of those provisions which lay down conditions for the exercise of concurrent legislative power. The second paragraph of Article 72 of the Basic Law specifies that in the concurrent field a need for regulation by Federal law must exist on one of three specific grounds, namely that a matter cannot be effectively regulated by the legislation of an individual *Länder*, that regulation by *Land* law might prejudice the interests of other *Länder* or of the people as a whole, or that Federal regulation is necessary for the maintenance of legal or economic unity, especially the maintenance of uniformity of living conditions. The concepts involved are certainly indeterminate and call for the exercise of political judgment; but since in other areas the Court has not hesitated to assess the presumed effects of legislation or clarify the contours of imprecise concepts in the constitution, it might be expected that it would make the attempt here too. Yet almost from the start it virtually abandoned control over these preconditions for exercise of the wide range of Federal concurrent powers. The need for Federal legislation is declared to be a matter for the discretion of the Federal legislator. Moreover, in one decision the Court appears to accept a need for regulation by Federal law when the latter is intended not merely to maintain but to promote uniformity of living conditions.[8]

This approach may be judged to demonstrate prudent judicial self-restraint, especially in the circumstances of West Germany, where public opinion, more than in most federal states, tends to object to marked local deviation from uniform conditions. Nevertheless, it deprived the *Länder* of their main constitutional defence against Federal enthusiasm for exploiting the extensive concurrent legislative powers to the full. And if in recent years there have been signs of a willingness on the part of the Federal Government to exercise legislative self-restraint and examine in individual cases whether uniform Federal regulation is really necessary, this is certainly not due to the influence of the *Bundesverfassungsgericht*.

Federal 'occupation of the field'

The position is quite different with the provision in the first paragraph of Article 72 of the Basic Law that the *Länder* have power to legislate in the concurrent field in so far as the Federation does not exercise its right to do so. An analysis of the relevant judgments reveal that, where it has had real room for manoeuvre, the Court has tended to take an exacting view of what was necessary for the Federal legislator to have 'occupied the field' and thus to leave room for legislation by the *Länder*. However, such judicial activity is of limited impact, since it can at any time be overtaken by an unmistakable Federal occupation of the field in question.

The Federal framework power

More significant are the Court's decisions relating to the right of the Federation under Article 75 GG to enact framework provisions in a number of fields. In the absence of any specification of what constituted a framework and how far it could go into detail, the Constitutional

Court, in an early dispute between the Federal Government and the Government of North-Rhine-Westphalia on the salaries of public officials,[9] ruled out any idea that this was a question of discretion like the conditions laid down for the exercise of the concurrent power. In its view, a Federal framework law cannot stand on its own but must be designed to be 'filled in' by *Land* legislation; although it is not restricted to basic principles, it must leave to the *Länder* an area which is of substance. This has in most subsequent decisions been reiterated to protect the *Länder's* scope for legislative activity, even though it is doubtful whether the Federal framework laws always correspond to the Court's requirements.

The executive competence

In the field of administrative powers, which under the German federal system may be regarded as the privileged domain of the *Länder*, the Constitutional Court has recognised the principle that the legislative competence of the Federation constitutes the outermost limit of its administrative powers. It has interpreted the principle of Article 30 of the Basic Law that all residual powers accrue to the *Länder*, which is specifically repeated with regard to the execution of Federal laws in Article 83, as applying equally to administration which does not consist of the implementation of legislation: thus the Federal Government in principle needs explicit constitutional authority for any kind of administrative activity. And it has been very restrictive in its approach to the possibility of so-called 'mixed administration' by Federal and *Länder* authorities. However, the concern of the Court with the administrative competence of the *Länder* has most frequently been in relation to the veto power of the *Bundesrat*.

The veto power of the Bundesrat

Although the *Bundesrat* is a central political institution which operates by majority vote, its composition is designed to give the *Länder* governments a substantial influence on Federal legislation: it is thus an important factor in the federal system. The Basic Law made a distinction between those bills which required the consent of the *Bundesrat* to become law and those cases where its objection could be overridden by an equivalent majority of the *Bundestag*. In practice, however, the *Bundesrat* was able, by broad interpretation, to extend the former category to cover a far greater range of legislation than had originally been foreseen. In general, a bill required consent if it affected the interests or duties of the

Länder or laid down administrative procedures for them in their function of implementing Federal legislation. The *Bundesrat*, however, took an expansionist view of what constituted administrative procedure and regarded the presence in a lengthy bill of a single clause requiring its consent as being sufficient to give it an absolute veto over the bill as a whole. In several cases (especially the judgment of 1958 on the constitutionality of the succession of laws renewing the Prices Act of 1948[10] the *Bundesverfassungsgericht* gave its blessing to this approach; and the Federal Government seemed to be able to live with this state of affairs, reaching the necessary political accommodation with the *Bundesrat*.

The change of *Bundestag* majority in 1969, however, brought about an entirely new situation, since for the first time the 'chamber of the *Länder*' began to be used as a weapon of opposition. Using its majority in the *Bundesrat*, the CDU/CSU succeeded on several occasions in extorting concessions from the SPD/FDP coalition. This took the question of the *Bundesrat*'s veto power out of the realm of pure federal disputes concerning general *Länder* interests and into the category of federal disputes with party-political implications. More specifically, it brought to a head the long-standing difference of opinion concerning the *Bundesrat*'s practice of regarding every later amendment of a law passed with its consent, even if it altered only provisions which, taken by themselves, would not have required consent, as being also subject to absolute veto. It was this point that was raised by the governments of Rhineland-Palatinate (CDU) and Bavaria (CSU), when they challenged the constitutionality of the Fourth Pensions Insurance Amendment Act – a piece of legislation which was highly controversial between the political parties – on the ground that it had been enacted without the consent of the *Bundesrat*. The decision of the Constitutional Court in this politically charged case[11] was reached by a narrow majority. It brought relief to the Federal Government by restricting the *Bundesrat*'s veto to amendments of provisions which themselves required consent: if a later amendment made no new inroad into the field of *Länder* powers, than it did not need to be 'sanctioned' anew by *Bundesrat* consent. And the Court roundly declared that the considerable increase in the number of bills requiring consent which would result from acceptance of the *Bundesrat*'s claims would be contrary to the Basic Law's intention of an equilibrium between all the bodies participating in the legislative process.

That this retreat from the Court's earlier expansionist approach to the veto rights of the *Bundesrat* was not irreversible was shown by the decision handed down in 1978 in response to the challenge by some Christian-Democratic *Länder* to the Federal law establishing a practically free choice between military service and the alternative community (or 'civilian') service.[12] The Court accepted their argument that although the amendment to the Military Service Act did not directly affect the administrative arrangements already made by the original Act with *Bundesrat* consent, the expected influx into the civilian service constituted a change in the scope of the Federal authority's executive responsibility and therefore fresh authorisation from the *Bundesrat* was required.

Inevitably, with the return in the 1980s to a concordance between the majorities in *Bundestag* and *Bundesrat*, the problem of the veto power has also lost much of its political drama. But it may safely be assumed that it will continue to be a legal and political issue in the future.

The federal principle and federal comity

If much of the Court's decision-making in the context of the Basic Law is necessarily of a relatively 'interstitial' nature, it remains now to consider the extent to which the Court has sought to transcend this role by appealing to general principles held to be immanent in the Constitution.

The most obvious such principle is that of the 'federal state' proclaimed by Article 20 of the Basic Law. Traditional German constitutional theory did not provide the Court with a clear-cut doctrine as to what were the necessary attributes of a federal state. But this did not prevent the Court, in its early years, from explicitly basing some of its findings on the 'federal principle' or the 'essence of the *Bundesstaat*'. Thus an early decision concerning horizontal financial equalisation[13] deduced from the federal principle a duty of mutual support incumbent on *Bund* and *Länder*, including a duty of solidarity on the part of the stronger *Länder* towards the weaker. This finding, which was all the more remarkable in that the text of the Basic Law already gave clear authority to the Federal Government to take *Länder* funds for the purposes of equalisation, was then mitigated by the inference from the same federal principle that such equalisation may not go so far as to effect a financial 'levelling' of the *Länder*. Another early case concerning Federal provisions for the allocation of resources for housing construction to the various *Länder*[14] also gave the Court an opportunity to appeal to the federal principle as establishing basic conditions for cooperation in the federal state. Thus a legislative requirement that the Federal Government should take measures in agreement with the *Länder* could only mean the consent of each and every *Länder*. The Court stresses that as members of the Federation, the *Länder* are equal in status and rights: they are not subject to the rule of majority decision-making which obtains in the sphere of the democratic principle, but rather to the unanimity principle, namely that no *Land* can be overruled by the other

Länder. This enthusiastic start was even followed by a short-lived flirtation with the concept of a 'tripartite federal state' whereby the *'Bundesstaat'* as a whole was composed of both the *Bund* (or *'Zentralstaat'*) and the *Länder*; in consequence the interests of the *Bund* in relation to the *Länder* by no means necessarily coincided with the interests of the whole. However, in 1961, the Court explicitly disowned the theory of the three tiers and in fact for a long time thereafter the federal principle itself seldom played a significant part in the decisions of the Constitutional Court, and then mostly in support of a conclusion reached by more conventional methods. It is only in more recent years that a modest revival may be observed, as will be seen below.

The role of the related principles of federal comity (*'Bundestreue'* or *'bundesfreundliches Verhalten'*) has been more prominent. This principle was explicitly derived by the Court from the notion of federalism, and it was held to create for the *Länder* in their relations with each other and with the 'greater whole', and for the Federation in its relations with the *Länder*, a duty in constitutional law to keep faith and cooperate sincerely to reach a common understanding.[15] The potential of such a doctrine was obviously considerable; indeed, it seemed to open hitherto unsuspected possibilities of judicial intervention in the political bargaining process within the federal system.

Having already delineated the contours of the comity principle, the Court was in a position to apply it to effect in the three most momentous federal judgments of its early years. This is therefore an appropriate point at which to take a closer look at each of these judgments, which demonstrate the undoubted impact which the Constitutional Court has had upon the German federal system.

The Concordat Case

This case, which was decided in 1957, came as the climax of a struggle between the conflicting claims of the foreign affairs power of the Federation and the internal legislative competence of the member States, such as is familiar from other federal systems. In *Missouri v Holland*, the US Supreme Court ruled that the treaty-making power of Congress extended also to matters which otherwise would not belong to the powers of Congress, and the High Court of Australia has adopted a similarly broad construction of the Federal Government's power to conclude and to implement treaties. In Canada, on the other hand, the Judicial Committee of the Privy Council took the view in the Labour Conventions Case of 1937 that the legislative power of 'performing' a treaty followed the normal allocation of powers for the class of subjects concerned.

The immediate object of the dispute in the German case was the Concordat signed by the German *Reich* with the Vatican in 1933, which among other things guaranteed separate church-controlled schools for all Roman Catholic children in Germany. For this reason, the Federal Government asked the Constitutional Court to strike down legislation of Lower Saxony virtually abolishing confessional education. The Court found that although the Concordat was still valid and binding, under the Basic Law education belonged to the exclusive powers of the *Länder*: an international obligation of the Federal Government arising from a treaty with a foreign power could not in itself give it the right to regulate the subject in question if it otherwise fell within the jurisdiction of the *Länder*.

In the light of the number and scope of international treaties in the modern world, the importance of this decision of principle protecting the position of the *Länder* can hardly be overestimated. But it left the fundamental problem of the gulf between the international obligations of the Federal Republic and the Federal Government's inability to ensure respect to them internally. It was here that the Court drew attention to the relevance of the duty of federal comity, which demanded special consideration by the members for the external interests of the Federation. Yet instead of drawing practical consequences from the doctrine – it might, for example have decided that the *Länder* had a duty in federal comity at least to respect international obligations of the Federal Republic originating from before the distribution of powers by the Basic Law – the Court preferred to leave the autonomy of the *Länder* in the education field unimpaired.

With an eye to the future, the Court could only declare: 'In the case of tension between Federal and *Land* interests, it must be left to an accommodation between *Bund* and *Länder* on a basis of equality to reach an acceptable settlement.' And interestingly, in the very same year a compromise was reached by the so-called 'Lindau agreement' whereby *inter alia* the contracting of international obligations by the Federal Government in fields of exclusive *Länder* powers was made conditional on the prior accent of the *Länder*. The successful functioning of the Lindau agreement in practice could indeed be seen as having vindicated the decision of the Court.

The Atomic Weapons Referendum Cases

In the course of the heated conflict between the Adenauer Government and the opposition SPD on the question of the rearmament of West Germany and its commitment to NATO, the *Bundestag* majority voted in favour of providing the German army with tactical nuclear weapons.

Predictably frustrated at federal level, the SPD tried to make use of the fact that it was in power in certain of the *Länder* to influence the course of events. Measures were passed in Hamburg and Bremen for the holding of advisory referendums on the question of support for or opposition to arming the *Bundeswehr* with atomic weapons, and this led to a case before the Constitutional Court, which established that although such referendums would not be binding on any government, they would constitute undue pressure on the *Bund* in a field of its exclusive competence.[16]

When a number of local authorities in Hesse decided to hold similar referendums and the *Land* Government refused to annul these decisions, the Federal Government took the matter to Karlsruhe and itself appealed to the principle of federal comity: given that the municipalities had interfered in the exclusive Federal sphere of defence, and that the Federal Government had no power of control over local authorities, the Government of Hesse was violating its duty of federal comity by failing to exercise its constitutional supervision of the observance of the Basic Law by the local authorities on its territory. In the event, the position of the Federal Government, and in particular the use of the doctrine of federal comity as the main basis of an important constitutional judgment, was endorsed by the Constitutional Court.[17]

The Television Case

The judgment delivered in 1961 in relation to the Adenauer Government's attempt to create a second television channel by founding the so-called 'German Television Ltd.' is probably the Constitutional Court's most celebrated and controversial decision.[18] It is neither necessary nor possible to relate all its details here. Suffice it to recall that after deciding (in contrast, for example, to the Australian High Court) that the Federal competence for 'Post and Telecommunications' encompassed only the technical sphere of transmission and not broadcasting as a whole, and *a fortiori* not the second television network just established by the Adenauer Government, the Karlsruhe judges launched into a massive attack on the way the Federal Government had treated the *Länder*. The way in which it had, on the principle of *'divide et impera'*, sought agreement only with those *Land* governments which it found politically congenial, intending to present the others with a *fait accompli*; the delaying of a response to new counter-proposals from the *Länder* so that it reached them after the new company had been established; the appointment of the Federal Minister of Justice as temporary trustee for the interests of the reluctant *Länder* – all these aspects of the Federal

Government's behaviour and tactics were declared by the Court to be incompatible with the requirements of federal comity.

Not surprisingly, the highly political argumentation and severity of tone of a rebuke which was purely incidental to the decision of a fairly clear-cut question of legislation and administrative powers under the Basic Law caused a sensation. Even granted the desirability of bringing home to the Federal Government that such arrogant conduct toward the *Länder* was inadmissible, it was doubtful whether such a reprimand should come in pseudo-legal terms from a court of law. The judgment would have been enough to confirm Dicey's worst fears, and it is understandable in view of the public controversy it unleashed that the constitutional judges thereafter drew in their horns. Nevertheless, not only has the judgment remained definitive as regards the lack of any Federal competence for domestic broadcasting, but it would be hard to find a similar example of Federal high-handedness towards the *Länder* since then.

The Television Judgment of 1961 was not only the high-point of the Constitutional Court's decision-making in federal matters; it also proved to be a watershed in its application of the doctrine of federal comity. Although the Court continued to refer to the general implications of the federal comity, there is no instance in the following decade and more of the principle being used, as previously, to mitigate or enhance the impact of a decision based on the letter of the Basic Law. To this extent its fate was similar to that of the federal principle itself. There may be several reasons for this change to a more modest and less creative role. Almost certainly, it is partly due to the Court's susceptibility to public and academic criticism following the Television Judgment: the political aspect of a constitutional court's decision-making makes it particularly dependent on maintaining a basis of public respect and acceptance. But another reason must now be considered, namely that the comity principle can most effectively be applied as a corrective in circumstances where governments are jealously guarding – or ruthlessly exploiting – their constitutional powers: its importance may have been much less obvious in the changed political circumstances of the 1960s, with the advent of 'cooperative federalism'.

Cooperative federalism and judicial review

The judgments of the Federal Constitutional Court considered above show that it has played a significant, indeed essential, part in the arbitration of the federal relationships. Nevertheless, if one looks at the substantial shifts which have occurred in the balance of the federal system since 1949, it is clear that many of the developments have passed the Court by. In a comparatively small and homogeneous country most of the changes have resulted from pressure for ever greater uniformity in the provision of government services, co-ordinated planning for efficient use of resources, and centralised oversight of public expenditure having regard to the needs of economic management. They have come about in a variety of ways.

Given the detailed and comprehensive nature of the Basic Law, the comparative ease with which it can be amended, and the German preference for explicit legal authorisation, one of the most obvious methods is amendment of the constitutional text. Either by simple addition to the catalogue of powers or (especially in the financial field) by more elaborate redrafting, a succession of amendments concentrated particularly in the years 1965–72 have consistently added to the powers of the Federation. Thus frequently where it was clear that the *Länder* had the Basic Law on their side, they themselves agreed to surrender competence or share it with the Federation, sometimes in fields as important as higher education, economic management and financial planning, and protection of the environment. When the *Länder*, in recognition of their own inability, particularly financial inability, to cope adequately with certain responsibilities, were prepared, even though reluctantly, to abdicate their powers, the possibility of defending their prerogatives by appeal to the Constitutional Court no doubt lost much of its relevance. This must go a long way towards explaining the dearth of federal disputes during the 1960s.

Even more important for its effect on judicial review in the federal system is the tendency, in tackling the complex and interrelated problems of modern government, to find a rigid demarcation of competences inadequate and constricting. Although West German federalism from its inception differed markedly from the classical federal model and exhibited a degree of interpenetration of competences and possibilities of mutual influence not found in Anglo-Saxon federations, it did not therefore fail to experience, in particularly intense form, the phenomenon of cooperative federalism. Despite their dubious legal status, a complex web of institutions of coordination and cooperation grew up, both between the *Länder*, in order to meet the need which became felt for as uniform a regulation as possible of certain areas falling within their competence, and between the *Bund* and *Länder* acting together. This development took place (at least until 1969) outside the constitutional framework and became one of the foremost characteristics of West German federalism. In practice, the Federal Government came increasingly to be accepted as a partner in cooperative undertakings, as even some of the fairly successful areas of inter-*Länder* cooperation laboured under rising costs.

In 1969, the ever more widespread *ad hoc* cooperative activity of *Bund* and *Länder* received in some fields the imprimatur of constitutional law with the introduction of 'joint tasks' in Articles 91a and 91b of the Basic Law, whose essence consists in joint planning and financing by *Bund* and *Länder* of projects falling within the field of competence of the latter. The integrated decision-making by planning committees consisting of representatives of the Federal and *Land* governments, the products of which are directly legally binding on the governments concerned, was a new phenomenon in a federal system. Moreover, since the Federal Government has 50 per cent of the votes in the planning committees and decisions are taken by 75 per cent majorities, it needed only to influence a bare majority of the *Länder* via party-political pressure or their dependence on financial aid in order to have its way. (This in spite of the principles enunciated in the early years by the Constitutional Court that as member states of the Federation the *Länder* enjoy equal status, so that among them only the unanimity principle, and not decision-making by majority vote, may be applied.)

Nevertheless, the consistent shift of power in the Federal Government's favour, which has taken place by both constitutional and paraconstitutional means, and the blurring of the previously clear boundary lines between the responsibilities of the two levels of government came about on the whole unaffected by judicial pronouncements.

To these developments must be added the emergence, as a result of the superior financial strength of the Federation, of an extensive system of Federal subsidisation of projects belonging to the domain of the *Länder*, much along the lines of the grants-in-aid familiar from other federal systems. This enabled the Federal Government to achieve a substantial influence over the priorities of *Land* expenditure by making its contribution conditional on the provision of a complementary (and often equal) sum by the *Land* concerned. Despite serious doubts about the constitutionality of so potent an instrument of Federal control, the issue was – perhaps understandably – never brought before the Karlsruhe Court by *Länder* increasingly dependent on Federal funds. And when in 1969 the practice was given constitutional legitimation by Article 104a, paragraph 4 of the Basic Law, it appeared to have been put to all intents and purposes beyond such challenge: the broad economic criteria laid down for Federal grants were unlikely to prove more justiciable than those for Federal concurrent legislation.

Nevertheless, a case taken to Karlsruhe by the Bavarian Government in 1972 showed that even in such apparently unfavourable circumstances judicial arbitration could still have an important part to play. It concerned precisely that field which had seemed so immune from judicial review: grants-in-aid. Giving judgment in 1975,[19] the Court exercised self-restraint in relation to the very general criteria stipulated in

Article 104a of the Basic Law for Federal investment aid and accepted that the disputed Federal law for the promotion of urban building (*'Städtebauförderungsgesetz'*) was designed to promote economic growth. But it seized the opportunity to make wide-ranging comments on the whole system of grants-in-aid and the vital influence of financial arrangements on the autonomy of the *Länder*. In particular, the requirement that the *Länder* accept certain conditions or controls as a prerequisite for receiving investment aid would, in the Court's view, violate the freedom of decision belonging to the members of a federation. The power of Federal subsidy must not be used as an instrument of manipulation of investment in order to promote the general objectives of the Federation in the *Länder*. On the contrary, it must have due regard to the investment plans of the *Länder* and do no more than fit them into a coherent overall pattern. Thus returning to the essential characteristics of the federal order as a source of specific findings, the Court used them here to develop guidelines and safeguards which even the constitutionally legitimated practice of grants-in-aid must respect. Together with another case in the following year on a special Federal aid programme for areas with structural problems, in which the Bavarian Government was also successful,[20] it shows the Court making a determined attempt to tackle one of the most intractable areas of federal relations and set limits to a practice threatening the balance of power between *Bund* and *Länder*.

The conclusion to be drawn is therefore twofold. First of all, the simultaneous expansion of cooperative federalism and Federal dominance shows that the potential for 'development' of the federal system relatively unaffected by the Constitutional Courts is very considerable. But secondly, if disenchantment grows with the results of cooperative federalism then resentment at its undoubted erosion of the political autonomy of the *Länder* may – especially in circumstances of increasing party-political polarisation, as in the 1970s – produce a greater willingness to take issues before the Constitutional Court. For, however much the practice of cooperative federalism may subject the federal division of powers to *ad hoc* agreement and coordination by the governments concerned, the ultimately competitive nature of the federal relationship remains.

Competitive federalism and the Court

That this competitive relationship also obtains between the *Länder* themselves was demonstrated in dramatic fashion by the recent challenge by six *Länder* Governments to the Federal law on financial equalisation. In many respects the spectacle was an unedifying one. The rich *Land* of Baden-Württemberg argued that in assessing the financial capacity of each *Land*, the Federal Government could only take revenues into account, but not the special expenditure needs of individual *Länder*. Others accepted that needs be included in the calculation, but claimed that those special burdens which the Federal legislator had taken into consideration (the special urban character of city-states and their responsibility for the upkeep of their ports, traditional structural problems of the Saarland, refugee problems in Schleswig-Holstein) had been arbitrarily selected and others ignored; some of the beneficiary *Länder* maintained, on the contrary, that their special burdens had not been taken *sufficiently* into account. North-Rhine-Westphalia, together with Hesse and the city-states, objected to the fact that only tax receipts in the strictest sense were considered, while revenues from other levies and dues – in particular Lower Saxony's oil revenues – were at most partially included: Lower Saxony, rejecting this, retorted that *if* such levies were included, account would have to be taken of similar levies which other *Länder* could impose in respect of their mineral wealth if they chose (a reference to coal in North-Rhine-Westphalia). Similar arguments were put forward about the so-called 'complemental grants' which could be made from Federal funds to the weak *Länder*. In short, the aim of each *Länder* was, on every possible count, to secure a larger slice of the cake for itself and/or to refute the arguments of the other applicant *Länder* which were trying to do the same.

This 'dog-bites-dog' situation might be considered the perfect illustration of Dicey's reproach that 'federalism substitutes litigation for legislation'. It might indeed be held – and was by some – that it was a clear invitation to the Constitutional Court to substitute its own political judgment for that of the legislature. Yet it must be remembered that there is no guarantee that the criteria adopted by the Federal Government for the apportionment of funds are objective – in so far as that is in fact possible. Not only is it not required (*et pour cause!*) to reach a negotiated agreement with all the *Länder*, but (understandably too) the criteria of horizontal financial equalisation do not even require the consent of the *Bundesrat*. In these circumstances, the availability of the Constitutional Court as a safety net is not unreasonable, though the task required of it may be demanding.

In the event, the Constitutional Court managed, in a fairly clear and convincing way, to sign-post the path through this particularly dense 'political thicket'[21]. And it did so with frequent reference to the requirements of the federal principle. Thus, having quoted the relevant passages of its early judgment on horizontal financial equalisation, it found that if only the tax revenues of the *Länder* were used as a criterion and their other revenues ignored, the interference with the autonomy of those *Länder* which were not contributors could no longer be justified by the federal principle of solidarity: such payments could only be based on the overall financial weakness of the other *Länder*. Broad discretion was left to the Federal legislator as to how to assess 'financial capacity', but – with the exception of the structural peculiarities of the city-states – the Court ruled that in this context the special needs of individual *Länder* were irrelevant. On the other hand, the Federal 'complemental grants' were indeed based on the relationship between revenues and expenditure needs: in the absence of further constitutional specification, the Federal legislator was free either to augment the financial capacity of the weaker *Länder* in general or to take special burdens into account or both.

On this basis, the Court found major parts of the relevant legislation to be unconstitutional and, so to speak, referred it back to the politicians with guidelines for another attempt. The judgment was on the whole received with a good grace. Not surprisingly, there was less ready acceptance of the concrete changes hammered out in lengthy negotiations and transformed into Federal legislation, even though the – for some *Länder* – bitter pill was sugared with an overall increase in the amount of complemental grants. Indeed, it is to be feared that the Constitutional Court may be confronted by the issue again. But if so, the fault can hardly be laid at its door.

Another problem which has become ever more acute over the years is the impact of European integration on the domestic federal relationship in the Federal Republic.[22] There is an obvious connection with the question of the foreign affairs power, but the potential impact on the balance of the federal system is far greater, given the mass of Community legislation which has to be digested by the national legal and political systems. Above all, in the decision-making process of the Community, it is the Federal Government that is in a privileged position *vis-á-vis* the *Länder*, even when the latter's sphere is at stake. In view of the consequent threat posed by the European integration process to the powers of the German *Länder*, it was no doubt inevitable that the issue should be taken to Karlsruhe. The application by the Bavarian Government to determine that by consenting to the proposed Community directive on broadcasting the Federal Government had violated its rights under Article 30 of the Basic Law thus confronts the Court once again with a most difficult challenge on a core issue of federal relations: at stake are, on the one hand, the traditionally jealously protected 'cultural sovereignty' of the *Länder* and, on the other, the Federal Government's freedom of activity in Community decision-making. The judgment will be eagerly awaited.

Conclusion

One way or another, most of the major problems of the federal relation-ship have come before the Constitutional Court. Sometimes they have been imbued with party-political antagonisms, which has ensured that they received widespread publicity. But it is arguable that the far more numerous cases of 'routine' demarcations of powers have, cumulatively, had just as great an effect in discouraging too carefree an approach by governments to the constitutional boundaries of their legitimate sphere of action. Moreover, as with most instruments of control, the impact is not limited to the actual cases decided, but awareness of the vigilance of the constitutional Court has a more general deterrent effect.

Given the balance of forces in the German federal system, and the centralising pressures to which it has been subject, it is natural that the *Länder* have felt the need to resort to judicial decision more often than the Federal Government. For the same reason, it is to be expected that any propensity of the Court to insist on strict observance of the wording and the spirit of the constitution will benefit the weaker element in the federal relationship. And indeed we have seen that on the whole – though not at all times and not on all questions (cf. the criteria for concurrent legislation) – the resolution of federal issues has tended to protect the position of the *Länder*.

The record of the Constitutional Court in federal matters hardly amounts to Dicey's 'predominance of the judiciary in the constitution', if by that is meant the inhibition of dynamic political development. The German federal system of today is no longer what it was in 1949. The Court has usually been at pains to leave room for political discretion and has recognised the limitations to the role of a court in controlling the natural interplay of political forces. Nevertheless, it has seldom failed, when given the opportunity, to direct the development of federal re-lations along constitutionally acceptable channels. It may safely be said that the German federal system would not be what it is today without the umpiring role of the Constitutional Court.

Notes

1. This chapter is largely based on the author's book, *Federalism and judicial review in West Germany*, Clarendon Press, Oxford (1981), which provides a more detailed analysis and further references.
2. K. Hesse. *Der unitarische Bundesstaat*, Muller, Karlsruhe (1966).
3. *Entscheidungen des Bundesverfassungsgerichts*, issued by the members of the Court, Mohr, Tübingen (1952–), Vol. 3, case number 407 (hereafter, BVerfGE 3, 407 etc.).
4. BverfGE 4, 7.

5. BverfGe 41, 344.
6. BVerfGE 67, 256.
7. BVerfGE 7, 29.
8. BVerfGE 13, 230.
9. BVerfGE, 4, 115.
10. BVerfGE 8, 274.
11. BVerfGE 37, 363.
12. BVerfGE 48, 127.
13. BVerfGE 1, 117.
14. BVerfGE 1, 299.
15. BVerfGE 1, 299.
16. BVerfGE 8, 104.
17. BVerfGE 8, 122.
18. BVerfGE 12, 205.
19. BVerfGE 39, 96.
20. BVerfGE 41, 291.
21. BVerfGE 72, 330.
22. See further Rudolf Hrbek's contribution to this volume.

5 German federalism and the challenge of European integration[1]

Rudolf Hrbek[*]

Throughout the history of the Federal Republic of Germany, now more than forty years old, the federal system has continually been subject to change and has proved to be very adaptable. Changes have taken place in response to a wide variety of economic, social and political challenges and have included both formal constitutional amendments and, above all, *ad hoc* responses as the federal structure has adapted to new circumstances.[2] Throughout this process the central principles of federalism have always been upheld. Since the mid-1980s discussion about the future of federalism in the Federal Republic has focused on the question of how progressive integration into the EC will affect the federal system and how this new and massive challenge is to be met.[3]

EC integration as a challenge for the German Länder and German federalism

An essential feature of German federalism is the fact that the *Länder* have the status of member states and are not merely territorial units acting as the administrative subordinates of central government. This has two main implications:

– Under the Basic Law, the *Länder* have sole responsibility for specific policy areas, including education and training, transport and environmental policy, media policy and structural economic policy at the regional level. The *Länder* have the right to make policies in these areas on an autonomous basis. As the federal nature of the system is

* The author would like to thank Caroline Clark for her translation of this chapter.

considered to be one of the inviolable principles of the constitution, and therefore cannot be overruled under the normal provisions for constitutional amendment, the legislative autonomy of the *Länder* cannot be reduced below a certain level, as this would, otherwise, endanger their independent political status.
 – Article 50 of the Basic Law stipulates that the *Länder* 'shall participate through the *Bundesrat* in the legislation and the administration of the Federation'. This means that the *Länder* have the constitutionally guaranteed right to participate in the public policy process.

In this context the *Länder* are faced with a dual challenge from the EC and its policies. Firstly, their freedom to make independent policies is reduced as the Community's activities expand. Secondly, they feel that they are given insufficient opportunity to take part in internal discussions and decision-making on EC matters and that their scope for doing so has been reduced further since the start of the 1980s. In the eyes of the *Länder*, these two problems represent a threat to the federal structure in that they place both their political autonomy and the established balance between *Bund* and *Länder* in jeopardy.

Incursions by the EC into the responsibilities of the Länder

While the EC is not a super-state attempting to remove or greatly reduce the status of its members as states in their own right, reducing them to mere administrative units, it is, however, much more than a traditional international organisation. It is a completely new type of international community to which its member states have transferred a whole range of political powers in certain designated areas. In these areas, the EC has a legal right to issue legislation binding on its member states. This right is based on:

 – treaty provisions which transfer responsibilities to the Community in areas such as agriculture, trade, competition and transport;
 – Article 100 of the EEC Treaty, which concerns the harmonisation of the legal regulations in areas which are important for the establishment and functioning of the Common Market; also, Article 100a of the EEC Treaty, which regulates the decision-making process for the establishment of the Single Market and, with a few exceptions, requires majority decisions in the Council of Ministers;
 – Article 235 of the EEC Treaty, which embodies a so-called *'Kompetenz-Kompetenz'* or, in other words, a sort of general authorization for Community regulations to be issued in areas where the Treaty has not specifically provided for powers of action.

On the basis of these powers, the Community has been active across a whole range of areas which has been extended considerably since the beginning of the 1980s. This extension of Community activity has meant that it has assumed powers in policy areas which, according to the constitutional distribution of the responsibilities in the FRG, are incumbent upon the *Länder*. Some of these policy areas are the sole responsibility of the *Länder*, while others impinge on their essential interests. The following list presents examples of cases where the *Länder* are particularly affected by EC activities.[4]

- Cultural, educational and training policy is one of the most important of the areas of responsibility of the *Länder*. The *Länder* are critical of the fact that the Community has been increasingly active in this field, with the effect of eroding their independent legislative powers. For example, measures taken by the Community to regulate training and access conditions for particular professions encroach upon these powers. The *Länder* are also critical of the fact that the Community has been active in certain matters of cultural and educational policy where there is no obvious need for regulation. Examples of this would include measures taken concerning the training of interpreters or plans to set up a Community-wide film academy.
- The attempts of the EC Commission to regulate broadcasting have produced a particularly negative response on the part of the *Länder*. Under German constitutional law, the regulation of broadcasting is an exclusive responsibility of the *Länder*. While the *Länder* concede that broadcasting can be seen as an economic activity with cross-border implications – which would normally justify EC intervention – they insist that the essential functions of broadcasting are cultural and social, and do not, therefore, require EC intervention.
- Health policy is a further responsibility of the *Länder* under the Basic Law. Here, the *Länder* are critical of cancer and AIDS-prevention programmes initiated by the Community. The *Länder* dispute the idea that the Community should be responsible for such matters at all and that there is any need for Community-wide action.
- The area of research policy is a further cause for criticism on the part of the *Länder*. They have warned that the Community is infringing directly or indirectly upon, and hence detracting from, the freedom of the *Länder* to develop their own policies in the field. They feel that measures taken by member states (and their constituent parts) ought still to be possible and should in no way be impeded.
- In the area of environmental policy, which was made a Community responsibility following the passing of the Single European Act of 1986, it is felt that the principle of subsidiarity should likewise be strictly observed. If the Community is to have any say in this area at

all, it should take into consideration the high environmental standards already attained in the FRG.
- The ability to conduct their own structural economic policy independently and thus to promote the regional economy is of particular
importance to the *Länder*. However, if the *Länder* give financial
support to individual companies as part of such a regional economic
policy, this inevitably has implications for the competitive conditions
of the market concerned. Such support is subject to regulation by the
Commission under the terms of the EC Treaties. Subsidies are only
admissible under certain conditions and with the consent of the
Commission. The *Länder* consider this regulatory framework to be a
serious encroachment upon their policy autonomy, and feel that
regional economic policy should remain an exclusive concern of the
Länder and that the Community should play a lesser role.

The above list demonstrates how the *Länder* are affected by EC policy
and why they are concerned both that their independent political status
is being undermined and, more generally, that the essence of the federal
system is being placed at risk. As an initial response, the *Länder* have
called for the EC to be less interventionist and to observe the principle of
subsidiarity more closely.[5] Accordingly, they feel that the Community
should only take action in areas where a real need has been established
for Community-wide regulations. Any Community measures which lack
a sufficient legal basis, as in the case of the measures taken in the area of
broadcasting, should be stopped altogether.

The limited basis for Länder *participation in EC decision-making*

The major criticisms of the *Länder* focus on the decision-making process
in the EC, which creates considerable problems for a federally struc-
tured member state like the Federal Republic. The Council of Ministers,
in which the FRG is represented by the Federal Government, remains
the most important legislative organ in the Community. As we have
seen, some of the decisions made in the EC directly impinge on areas
which are the sole responsibility of the *Länder*, while others affect their
essential interests. This means that the Federal Government has a part in
making decisions externally in the Council which extend beyond its
internal powers under the Basic Law. To this extent the Community fails
to take into account the federal structure of the FRG. The Treaties
ensure that each member state is represented by its central government,
but fail to take into account the different ways in which opinion is
formed internally and, in particular, which bodies are involved in the
internal decision-making process.

For these reasons, the *Länder* have consistently demanded, ever since the Community was set up, that they be given far-reaching rights to participate in internal discussions and decision-making processes concerning EC matters.[6] In this way they have sought to guarantee that their interests are properly taken into account. In cases where the EC Treaties already provide for or permit decisions to be made at Community level in policy areas which the *Länder* consider to be within their field of responsibility, then it is felt that their influence on such decisions must be assured. The following two sections provide a description of the institutions, procedures and activities through which the *Länder* have attempted to improve and strengthen their involvement in European policy-making. The first deals with the period up to 1986–7 and the second with the period since then, during which the *Länder* have both succeeded in strengthening and legally guaranteeing their right of involvement and in intensifying considerably their own direct and independent EC activities.

Länder involvement in European policy-making up to 1986–7

Ever since the Community was founded, the *Länder* have repeatedly called for as extensive and effective powers as possible to participate in internal decision-making on EC affairs, justifying their demands by the fact that, as constituent parts of the federation, they are directly affected by EC activities. Although the Federal Government has always been sympathetic towards their demands, it has been less than generous in creating opportunities to allow for *Länder* involvement. The Federal Government has justified this in constitutional terms by referring to Article 32 of the Basic Law, which gives it the right to represent the Federal Republic abroad, and also to Article 24, which empowers the federation to transfer sovereign powers to intergovernmental institutions (the so-called power of integration). In more practical political terms, the Federal Government has justified its stance by pointing to the various functional and political demands created by EC integration which would make it impossible to subject European policy-making in the EC institutions to the approval of individual *Länder* or even to the approval of the *Bundesrat*. The Federal Government did, however, stress that it would without fail observe the principle of 'federal comity' (*Bundestreue*) in all decisions concerning European policy and that it would, in this way, take into account the interests of the *Länder*.

In view of their differing opinions on the constitutional situation, the Federal Government and the *Länder* have tended to adopt an *ad hoc* approach by devising and progressively extending rules and procedures which enable the *Länder* to take part in the internal decision-making process on EC affairs. These rules and procedures incorporate both formal and informal types of participation.[7]

The Bundesrat *procedure*

According to the Act of Ratification of the Treaty of Rome of 1957, the Federal Government is obliged to make available information on EC matters, and the *Bundesrat* is entitled (as is the *Bundestag*) to receive such information. Accordingly, the Federal Government has to pass on any of the Commission's proposals for regulations and directives to the *Bundesrat* as soon as the Council of Ministers receives them. The *Bundesrat* can then discuss these proposals and make recommendations to the Federal Government. If important sections of a draft are changed as it proceeds through the organs of the EC, then the draft must be submitted once again to the *Bundesrat* in its new form. While the Federal Government is not bound to act on the recommendations of the *Bundesrat*, it must, in accordance with the principle of federal comity, take them into account when formulating a viewpoint and when conducting negotiations in EC bodies. Moreover, at the request of the *Bundesrat*, the Federal Government supplies information on decisions made by the Council as well as on any deviations from the *Bundesrat*'s recommendations.

This procedure for passing on information has made it possible for the *Länder* to have an effective influence on internal decision-making on EC matters. This is because what was conceived merely as a supply of information to the *Bundesrat* has, in practice, developed into a regular and fairly intensive exchange of opinions between the Federal Government and the *Bundesrat* and, hence, the *Länder* governments. And as the expertise and administrative experience of the *Länder* has been made available through this form of communication, it has also been a useful and valuable practice for the Federal Government, not least because it is usually up to the *Länder* to implement EC decisions internally. Both those involved and informed observers generally view this procedure in a favourable light, although the *Länder* still do not feel that it fully meets their demands for an effective voice in EC policy.

The Länder *Observers at the EC*

The institution of *Länder* Observer was set up as early as 1956 during the negotiations on the EEC Treaty. His task is to gather information on EC affairs and to pass on such information to the *Bundesrat*, to the *Länder* governments and to the organs of cooperative federalism (and, in particular, to cross-*Länder* ministerial conferences). The *Länder* Observer attends the sessions at the Federal Economics Ministry where Federal Government directives to the Permanent Representation in Brussels are prepared, and also attends sessions of the Councils of Ministers and its committees. Moreover, the Observer has a great number of informal contacts in Brussels and is therefore centrally placed within the inner-EC information network. The Observer's activities are certainly useful for the *Länder* but, in view of the extremely modest staffing levels and resources of his office, his effectiveness is limited.

The participation of Länder *representatives in EC committees*

This form of *Länder* participation emerged without a firm legal basis and has evolved in a completely *ad hoc* fashion. It involves the participation of representatives of the *Länder* in the Federal Government's delegations to EC committees. Their function is twofold. On the one hand, they offer their expertise as members of the Federal Government's delegation, which has often been useful for the Federal Government as well; and on the other hand, they have gained an opportunity to represent the specific interests of the *Länder*. Their status is not that of the Federal Government's representative abroad, but of *Land* representative within the FRG. This has resulted in practice in the presence of *Länder* representatives in many different committees.

The procedure for Länder *participation*

With the Community's activities on the increase in the mid-1970s, the *Länder* began to be affected more and more by EC legislation and felt that the means of participation open to them – the *Bundesrat* procedure in particular – were no longer sufficient. They therefore sought to introduce a statutory guarantee for their right of involvement in decision-making on EC matters. The result was the so-called procedure for *Länder* participation, which was introduced at the end of 1979 following negotiations between *Bund* and *Länder*, conducted in an exchange of correspondence between the Federal Chancellor and the Chairperson of the Conference of Ministers.

This agreement underlined first and foremost the obligation of *Bund* and *Länder* to cooperate closely and in good faith on EC projects which fall within the exclusive legislative competence of the *Länder*, or which affect their essential interests. In comparison to the *Bundesrat* procedure, the obligation to pass on information was extended to include information concerning the Commission's initiatives and bills before these were formally submitted to the Council. The Federal Government expected that this procedure would enable the *Länder* to reach and present a unified viewpoint within an appropriate period of time, thereby taking into consideration the aims and needs of the Federal Government's foreign and integration policy. The agreement stipulated that the government could only deviate from the *Länder* viewpoint for 'reasons of foreign and integration policy which force it to do so' and was obliged to provide reasons for doing this. At the request of the *Länder*, the Federal Government was, if possible, to draft in two *Länder* representatives to the negotiations of the advisory committees of both the Council of Ministers and the Commission. A new paragraph (85a), setting out regulations for this new procedure, was added to the Common Rules of Procedure of the Federal Ministries. Finally, the *Länder* set up so-called 'Common Offices' in different policy areas to act as points of contact for each of the relevant ministries of the Federal Government.

The new procedure differs from the *Bundesrat* procedure in that each *Land* now has an equal voice – rather than a majority vote in the *Bundesrat*, unanimous agreement between the *Länder* must be achieved. However, the new procedure has, in general, been poorly received for several reasons.[8] One of these has been the difficulties of coordination created by the need to secure consensus between the *Länder*. Others have included the problem of maintaining two procedures alongside one another, and, in particular, the lesser effectiveness of the new procedure. Generally, the older *Bundesrat* procedure has been more effective due to the fact that the *Bundesrat* is a firmly established institution with a good and extremely efficient administrative infrastructure and many proven channels of communication at its disposal.

The treatment of EC matters within the framework of Bund–Länder *coordination*

In addition to the special institutions and procedures outlined above, which are designed to secure *Länder* involvement in EC matters, the *Länder* also have access to other channels of influence via the established framework of their relations with the *Bund*, which, as Uwe Leonardy shows in Chapter 3 of this volume, are characteristic of the federal structure of the FRG. As EC concerns have an impact on most areas of policy, they are automatically dealt with, to some extent, in the institutions and procedures of *Bund–Länder* coordination. This applies to cross-*Länder* ministerial conferences as well as to the special teams of EC experts in each of the *Länder* ministries and also, of course, to the Conference of Minister-Presidents. This intermeshing of policies is illustrated particularly well by the example of regional policy: internally, regional policy is, in part, one of the Joint Tasks, which *Bund* and *Länder* carry out and finance together. EC regional policy adds another dimension, designed to complement the jointly determined national policy of *Bund* and *Länder*.

Independent EC activities of the Länder

As well as the variety of means of involvement already described, the *Länder* have increased their direct input into EC matters. This includes the political contacts of *Land* politicians and authorities with Community institutions in Brussels, in particular with the EC Commission. Another form of direct action on the part of the *Länder* is represented in the influence of the Missions of the *Länder* in Bonn. Most of these have expressly been given the task of dealing with EC matters. They act as points of contact for EC affairs in the West German capital which companies and all sorts of organizations from each *Land* can approach. Finally, mention should also be made in this context of the efforts of *Länder* parliaments to take part in discussions and decision-making concerning EC matters whenever *Länder* interests are at stake. *Länder* parliaments are becoming increasingly involved in EC matters, dealing with individual policy areas where the EC and its policies are involved, and also regularly initiating EC debates. Once again, the intermeshing of the policies of the Community, member states and sub-national territorial units can be seen in such activities of the *Länder* parliaments.[9]

New forms of activity and participation of the *Länder* in EC affairs subsequent to the Single European Act (SEA)

Following protracted and difficult debates between the member states concerning the reform and development of the Community, additions and amendments were eventually made to the EC Treaties in the form of the SEA. While the SEA falls short of many of the more far-reaching demands and expectations arising from years of discussion on reform in the EC, it does nevertheless represent a step forward in the process of integration.[10] The EC member states came to an agreement that the Single Market should be completed by the end of 1992; most decisions in this respect can be taken by a qualified majority in the Council. The member states committed themselves to the aim of convergence in economic and monetary policy as a precondition for the establishment of economic and monetary union. They added research and technological development and environmental problems to the Community's area of responsibility, added declarations of intent in the area of social policy and resolved that redistributive measures in favour of weaker member states should be taken via a reform of the Structural Fund. While the German *Länder* welcomed this step towards integration, they did at the same time demand that their interests and those of the federal system of the FRG be taken into account.

The expansion and legal underpinning of the rights of participation of the Länder

With the acceleration of the integration process and the deepening of the Community, the *Länder* quite rightly expected that EC policy would affect them to an even greater extent. Therefore, they took advantage of the ratification of the SEA to strengthen their rights of participation in internal decision-making on EC affairs and, in particular, to have these rights guaranteed in legislation. As the Federal Government also considered the Act of Ratification to be a law requiring the consent of the *Länder*, the *Länder* were able to negotiate from a relatively strong position. They formulated common demands, irrespective of the party political differences of the various *Länder* governments, and presented them to the Federal Government. Discussions between the Federal Government and the *Länder* continued throughout the whole of 1986 so that the SEA ratification procedure was not concluded in the FRG until the end of that year.

The end result of this process of negotiation was incorporated in Article 2 of the Act of Ratification,[11] and contains the following provisions:

– Firstly, the Federal Government's obligation to pass on information was greatly extended. The Federal Government must give the *Bundesrat* 'as early as is possible comprehensive information concerning all EC projects which could be of interest to the *Länder*'. For only if the *Länder* know in good time exactly what form future EC regulations will take, do they have a real chance of ensuring that their concerns are taken into account and, wherever possible, carried through.
– The right of the *Länder* to have a say in decision-making is greatly enhanced by the fact that the Federal Government is now obliged to 'give the *Bundesrat* an opportunity to comment, within an appropriate period of time, on decisions which, wholly or in part, affect legislative areas for which the *Länder* are exclusively responsible, or which affect the essential interests of the *Länder*, before giving its consent to such decisions at EC level'. It is therefore possible for the

Länder to put across their views not only in cases where the area in question falls within their exclusive competence, but also when their essential interests are affected.

– The Federal Government is further obliged to take the *Bundesrat's* comments into account when conducting negotiations. This is laid down as follows: 'In cases where a viewpoint impinges on legislative areas which are the sole responsibility of the *Länder*, the Federal Government may only deviate from this viewpoint for irrefutable reasons of foreign and integration policy. Moreover, when considering a particular matter, it must take account of the interests of the *Länder* as presented by the *Bundesrat*'. Anyone familiar with EC decision-making procedures in the Council will know that the individual governments are nearly always forced to make concessions on their original aims at the negotiating table as they have to take the interests of other member states into consideration. This applies equally for the Federal Government, which can therefore be forced, in the course of negotiation, to depart from the position favoured by the *Bundesrat*. This problem is dealt with in the Act of Ratification as follows: 'Whenever the Federal Government deviates from a *Bundesrat* standpoint concerning a legislative matter which is the sole responsibility of the *Länder* . . . the Federal Government must inform the *Bundesrat* of the decisive reasons for this.' The introduction of this obligation to justify its actions is intended to make it more difficult for the Federal Government to deviate from the *Länder* viewpoint, i.e. the majority view in the *Bundesrat*, during negotiations.

– The demand by the *Länder* for their own civil servants to be allowed to take part in negotiations in EC committees, as a means of providing and securing a particularly effective representation of their *Länder* interests, was dealt with in the following provision: 'In cases where the *Bundesrat* is to be given an opportunity to comment, *Land* representatives are . . . upon request, to be brought into negotiations in the Commission's consultative committees in so far as this can be arranged by the Federal Government.' The reservation expressed in the last sentence takes into account the fact that it is not always possible for the Federal Government to appear at negotiations with a disproportionately large delegation and that it must take the interests and sensitivities of its partners into consideration.

Subsequent to the adoption of the Act of Ratification, the Federal and *Länder* governments entered detailed discussions on ways in which the *Länder* are to receive an adequate flow of information and on their participation via the *Bundesrat*. These discussions resulted in the conclusion of an Agreement.[12] This Agreement also formed the basis for the necessary changes made to the *Bundesrat's* rules of procedure, in particular the insertion of a new Section IVa.[13]

The most important point in the amended rules of procedure,[14] passed on 10 June 1988, is the introduction of a special chamber for EC bills. The EC Chamber is a constitutional novelty as it is not only an advisory committee, but also an independent body with decision-making powers (unlike all the other *Bundesrat* committees). EC Chamber decisions have the same force as decisions reached by the plenary session of the *Bundesrat*. The following considerations formed the basis of the establishment of this new institution:

– As EC bills must often be dealt with rapidly and the *Bundesrat* does not meet in plenary session frequently enough for this, the EC Chamber is designed to enable prompt responses on the part of the *Länder* through the *Bundesrat*.

– *Bundesrat* viewpoints are intended to be taken into account by the Federal Government in its negotiation stance in the EC committees. As success in negotiations can be jeopardized if a state's viewpoints and aims are revealed prematurely, discussions in the EC Chamber can be closed to the public, unlike *Bundesrat* plenary sessions.

This series of regulations, which was incorporated into the Act of Ratification of the SEA, enabled the *Länder* to improve considerably their right of involvement in internal decision-making on EC affairs and, most important of all, to have these rights incorporated in the statute book. The question remains, however, whether these regulations would stand up in practice and whether the *Länder* would really be able to increase their influence on EC decisions. Only after several years of experience will it be possible to answer this question and to make an overall assessment of the new procedures. Initial impressions would seem to suggest the following:[15]

– The quality and quantity of information passing through to the *Länder* via the *Bundesrat* has improved considerably. Around 10,000 items of information are received each year, although about 75 per cent of these are purely technical. Nevertheless, this leaves approximately 2,500 items which relate to substantial Community projects. On each of these, a decision must be made as to whether the *Bundesrat* should put forward a viewpoint on the particular proposal.

– The sheer quantity of items awaiting decision poses the problem of how they are to be processed. At the outset, the Committee for EC Affairs in the *Bundesrat* selects a sample of items of which it feels a *Bundesrat* viewpoint should be put forward. Then, each individual *Land* can add to this sample on the basis of a decision taken by its Cabinet, as can all the other *Bundesrat* committees (in which civil servants predominate). The matters thus selected are then passed on to the relevant *Bundesrat* committee, while the Committee for EC Affairs remains in overall charge.

- Once the *Bundesrat* has come to a decision on its viewpoint, this can still be amended if the course of negotiations in the EC committee so requires. Each *Land* can call for such an amendment.
- Up until spring 1990, the EC Chamber had only been convened twice. This would tend to suggest, as an interim conclusion, that EC matters can be dealt with within the routine work of the *Bundesrat*.
- Finally, *Land* representatives who are drafted in to Federal Government delegations to EC committees are nominated by the *Bundesrat*. This means that the *Länder* must reach agreement on this, which up to now has generally been achieved without any difficulties.

This must, however, be seen essentially as a preliminary assessment, which will surely need revision and, possibly, complete reconsideration as these procedures 'mature' over the coming years.

The intensification of the independent EC activities of the Länder

The *Länder* were not satisfied with strengthening their formal rights of participation in EC affairs, as described above; they have therefore also intensified their independent EC activities.

- Particularly significant in this respect has been the setting up of so-called *Land* Information Offices in Brussels. All of the *Länder* set up such offices in the period from 1985 to 1987.[16] At the outset, the Federal Government was critical, posing the question whether these offices were to become instruments of a 'secondary foreign policy' of the *Länder*.[17] Within a very short time, this question became obsolete[18] and the offices are now seen in a much less critical light as *Land* institutions designed to carry out the purely practical function of passing on information. All these offices have very similar functions. Two examples will give an indication of the nature and scope of their activities. Firstly, the functions of the Saarland Information Office are as follows.[19]
  - 'Its function is to pass on and to process information. It is to provide information on the Commission's and other EC institutions' activities to the *Land* authorities, to the local government institutions, to companies and to Universities. Also, with the help of the Office, informative events and talks are to be organised in Brussels, Bonn and in the Saarland.

- The Office is committed to stimulating the economy. Upon request, it is the Office's duty to support individual companies in making contacts in the Benelux area and with EC institutions.
- The Office helps with work on specific projects. In the last few months alone, 122 applications and a further 54 preliminary applications were received from within the Saarland, which had to be prepared in the correct manner and within set deadlines in order to proceed through the rather cumbersome bureaucracy, and which then had to be monitored in their path through the various bodies involved in the EC decision-making process.
- The Office organises exhibitions, concerts and representative events to promote a better picture of the Saarland and its people.
- The Office provides a forum for discussion on topics such as 'Saar-Lor-Lux' cooperation and on current EC topics, in which representatives of the EC institutions, of interest groups and other interested parties involved in politics and economics in Brussels all take part.'

Secondly, the functions of the Bavarian Information Office have been summarized as follows.[20]

- 'Informing the Bavarian state government of developments taking place in EC matters and in the European Parliament;
- Advising and supporting the Bavarian economy in its contacts with the EC;
- Providing a point of contact for public and private institutions from Bavaria;
- Preparing information visits by members of the Bavarian state government, the Bavarian *Landtag* and the Bavarian Senate to Brussels;
- Public relations work.'

- The *Land* Information Offices have now become established as one of the many actors and institutions which have set down roots around the network of EC institutions in Brussels, and which constitute a part of the increasingly complex system of communications in the EC.
- The Missions of the *Länder* in Bonn, which were already concerned with EC affairs before 1986–7, have since intensified their activities in this field. Such activities include, for example, arranging events on EC themes.
- The institutions of cooperative federalism also include EC topics in their agendas more and more frequently; this is true of meetings of the Conference of Minister-Presidents, as well as of various Conferences of the *Länder* Ministers, which cover a wide range of

policy areas. This is a clear sign of the extent to which member states' policies – and for the Federal Republic that also includes those of the *Länder* – are intermeshed with Community policies.

– The *Land* governments have intensified their efforts to adapt their staffing and procedures to meet the new opportunities to participate in decision-making and to exploit these to their greatest advantage. Thus, in the *Länder* governments, individual civil servants are employed exclusively to deal with EC affairs, whether as EC consultants in individual ministries or as EC policy coordinators for a particular *Land* government in its ministries. EC matters are also being included increasingly in training and retraining programmes for *Land* civil servants.

– Finally, the *Länder* parliaments are now more intensively concerned with EC affairs than previously. Thus, since March 1989, the *Land* government of Baden-Württemberg has been keeping the *Landtag* informed on a regular basis about EC projects of political importance, so providing the *Landtag* with an opportunity to formulate a viewpoint on such matters. In a whole range of cases the *Landtag* has then requested the *Land* government to put forward certain viewpoints in the course of *Bundesrat* discussions. The *Land* government subsequently informs the *Landtag* how it acted in the *Bundesrat*. Finally, more and more motions relating to EC affairs are being submitted to the *Land* government by individual parliamentary party factions. The relevant ministry then makes a statement on each of these motions. In this area, as elsewhere, more time is needed before a conclusive assessment of the activities of the *Länder* parliaments can be made. It is, however, already clear that the *Länder* parliaments are making an effort to take part in discussions on EC affairs which affect the interests of their *Länder*.

Perspectives for the federal system of the FRG

As has been shown in detail above, the German *Länder* have reacted to the challenges of EC integration in two ways. Firstly, they have intensified their independent, direct activities concerning EC matters; the *Länder* governments, without doubt, play the dominant role here,[21] but the *Länder* parliaments are also attempting to make their mark as participants in the EC decision-making process. Secondly, the *Länder* have successfully sought statutory guarantees for their rights of participation in internal discussions and decision-making on EC matters. They – or to be more explicit, the *Länder* governments – have certainly succeeded in strengthening their position in relation to the Federal Government. The new participatory procedures mean that, since the SEA and the new regulations of the Act of Ratification of the SEA came into force, the Federal Government and the *Länder* have, through the *Bundesrat*, co-operated in EC affairs more intensively than ever before. The agreement of the Federal Government and the *Länder* on these new procedures show that, once again, *Bund* and *Länder* have succeeded in redefining the balance between the two levels of government in the federal system which is crucial for the success of federalism. The consensus between *Bund* and *Länder* confirms that both are committed to the principle of federal comity. This indicates that the federal system has yet again proved to be both dynamic and capable of adapting to new circumstances.

These new rules and procedures together constitute a framework within which the status of the *Länder* as component parts of the federation can be maintained now and in the future, and within which the federal structure of the FRG can remain unimpaired by further EC integration. The demand of the *Länder* for the Community to restrict its initiatives and activities and to observe consistently the principle of subsidiarity is a stance shared by the Federal Government. There are clear indications that the significance of the principle of subsidiarity is also understood and valued in the EC Commission. In discussions on the future of Europe in the last two or three years, the concept of a 'Europe of Regions' has become increasingly prominent.[22] This term expresses above all the desire to look more and more to territorial units below the level of the EC member states and to strengthen their political significance. To this extent, these tendencies correspond with the aims of the German *Länder*.[23]

In December 1989 four of the *Länder* governments put forward a motion in the *Bundesrat* to make an amendment to the constitution;[24] They demanded that Article 24, which enables the *Bund* to transfer sovereign powers to intergovernmental institutions, be amended in such a way that laws concerning the transfer of sovereign rights to the EC would require the consent of the *Bundesrat*. Moreover, it was proposed that the right of the *Länder* to participate in EC decision-making, incorporated in the Act of Ratification, should also be guaranteed in the constitution. As a constitutional amendment requires a two-thirds majority in both *Bundestag* and *Bundesrat*, it was always rather unlikely that the motion would be successful. Indeed, it was rejected by the Federal Government on 13 June 1990.[25] It is probable for the time being that the status quo will prevail. Only when sufficient experience has been gained with the new procedures would it be appropriate to give thought to how the federal system could be adapted further to accommodate the realities and the needs of EC integration.

Notes

1. The author has been working on the subject of this chapter since the mid-1970s: see his article 'Politikverflechtung macht an den Grenzen nicht halt. Auswirkungen der EG-Mitgliedschaft auf die föderative Ordnung der Bundesrepublik Deutschland', in *Der Bürger im Staat* (1979), 38–43. The following exposition is based on six later articles by the author: 'Doppelte Politikverflechtung: Deutscher Föderalismus und Europäische Integration. Die deutschen Länder im EG-Entscheidungsprozeß', in Rudolf Hrbek and Uwe Thaysen (eds), *Die Deutschen Länder und die Europäischen Gemeinschaften*, Nomos Verlagsgesellschaft, Baden-Baden (1986), 17–36: 'Die deutschen Länder in der EG-Politik', *Außenpolitik* (1987), 120–32 (the English version 'The German Länder and the European Community' was published in *Außenpolitik. German Foreign Affairs Review* (1987), 120–33); 'Bundesländer und Regionalismus in der EG', in Siegfried Magiera and Detlef Merten (eds), *Bundesländer und Europäische Gemeinschaft*, Hochschule Speyer series, vol. 103, Berlin (1988), 127–49; 'Die Beteiligung der deutschen Länder an den innerstaatlichen Beratungen und Entscheidungen in EG-Angelegenheiten (insbesondere im Licht von Artikel 2 EEA-Gesetz und der Bund-Länder-Vereinbarung)', *Vorträge, Reden und Berichte aus dem Europa-Institut der Universität des Saarlandes*, no. 117 (1988); 'The German Länder and the European Community: towards a real federalism?' in Wolfgang Wessels and Elfriede Regelsberger (eds), *The Federal Republic of Germany and the European Community: The Presidency and beyond*, Bonn (1988), 215–30; 'Die Bundesländer und die EG', in *Projekt Europa. Die Verantwortung der EG für Europa und ihre Rolle in der Welt*, Landeszentrale für politische Bildung North-Rhine Westphalia, Paderborn (1989), 203–19. The chapter in this volume was translated by Caroline Clarke.
2. Hartmut Klatt gives a good, precise overview of this in his 'Reform und Perspektiven des Föderalismus in der Bundesrepublik Deutschland. Stärkung der Länder als Modernisierungskonzept', in *Aus Politik und Zeitgeschichte* (1986), 3–21. A more detailed account can be found in the special edition of *Publius. The Journal of Federalism*, **19** (1989), on 'Federalism and intergovernmental relations in West Germany: a 40th year appraisal' (ed. Arthur B. Gunlicks).
3. Two recent anthologies give detailed information on this whole question: Hrbek and Thaysen (1986); Magiera and Merten (1988). See also Sekretariat des Bundesrates (ed.), *Bundesrat und Europäische Gemeinschaft. Dokumente*, Bonn (1988), which provides a comprehensive documentation of developments up to and including September 1988.
4. Examples of how the *Länder* were affected in earlier years can be found in the following three publications: Hans Eberhard Birke, *Die deutschen Bundesländer in den Europäischen Gemeinschaften*, Berlin (1973); Karlheinz Oberthür, 'Die Bundesländer im Entscheidungssystem de EG', in *Integration* (1978), 58–65; Rudolf Morawitz, *Die Zusammenarbeit von Bund und Ländern bei Vorhaben der Europäischen Gemeinschaft*, Bonn (1981). During the debates on the ratification of the SEA in 1986, representatives of several *Land* governments provided a large number of examples of the situation at

that time; see *Sitzungen des Bundesrates*, 21 February 1986 and 16 May 1986. Examples of how the *Länder* have been affected by EC measures more recently are given by Michael Borchmann, 'Die EG im Brennpunkt politischer Aktivitäten der Bundesländer', in *Die Öffentliche Verwaltung* (1988) 623–33.

5. On 19 May 1988 the Heads of Government of the *Länder* met the President of the EC Commission, Jacques Delors, in Bonn for an exchange of opinions. During this meeting, Franz-Josef Strauß, the then Chairperson of the Conference of Minister-Presidents, presented the viewpoint of the *Länder* as to how their interests should be upheld without detracting from the development of the EC.

6. See the summary in Günter Jaspert, 'Der Bundesrat und die europäische Integration', *Aus Politik und Zeitgeschichte* (1982), pp. 17–32.

7. The following account is based on the works of Jaspert, Morawitz, Oberthür und Hrbek. See notes 1, 3 and 5.

8. A convincing evaluation of this procedure can be found in Ilva Hannaleck and Wolfgang Schumann, 'Die Beteiligung der Länder an der EG-Politik des Bundes. Probleme und Alternativen', *Zeitschrift für Parlamentsfragen* (1983), 362–71.

9. Eberhard Grabitz, Otto Schmuck, Sabine Steppat, Wolfgang Wessels and others have commented on the use of the term 'Verflechtungssystem' ('intermeshing system') in *Direktwahl und Demokratisierung. Eine Funktionenbilanz des Europäischen Parlaments nach seiner ersten Wahlperiode*, Bonn (1988), pp. 58–77. Fritz W. Scharpf points to the problems and consequences of the intermeshing of policies, including the tendency towards immobilism and stagnation. See Fritz Scharpf, 'Die Politikverflechtungsfalle: Europäische Integration und deutscher Föderalismus im Vergleich', *Politische Vierteljahresschrift* (1985), 325–56.

10. See Rudolf Hrbek, 'EC reform inch by inch', *Intereconomics* (1986), 130–6; Werner Weidenfeld, 'Die Einheitliche Europäische Akte'. *Außenpolitik* (1986), 375–83. See also the special SEA edition of *Integration* (1986).

11. Printed in *Bundesgesetzblatt* (BGBl) (1986), II, 1104.

12. This agreement is printed in a documentary collection published by the *Bundesrat* Secretariat (see note 3).

13. The new text is printed in *BGBl* (1988) I. 857. Reasons for the amendments are given in *Bundesrats-Drucksache* 230/88.

14. Information on these amendments is provided in Horst Risse, 'Vorlagen der Europäischen Gemeinschaft im Bundesrat. Zur Ergänzung der Bundesratsgeschäftsordnung', *NJW* (1988), 2780–1.

15. The Director of the *Bundesrat* and a civil servant in the *Bundesrat* Secretariat have made an initial assessment. See Georg-Berndt Oschatz and Horst Risse, 'Bundesrat und Europäische Gemeinschaft. Neue Verfahrensregeln der Bundesrats-Geschäftsordnung für EG-Vorlagen', *Die Öffentliche Verwaltung* (1989), 509–19.

16. Stefan Schmidt-Meinecke gives an account of the establishment of these *Länder* Offices in Brussels in his 'Bundesländer und Europäische Gemeinschaft. Entwicklung und Stand der Länderbeteiligung im europäischen Einigungsprozeß', *Speyerer Forschungsberichte*, **59** (1987). 100–10.

17. See Klaus-Otto Nass, '"Nebenaußenpolitik" der Bundesländer', *Europa-Archiv* (1986), 619–28, and Ottokar Hahn, 'EG-Engagement der Länder: Lobbyismus oder Nebenaußenpolitik?', in Hrbek and Thaysen (1986), 105–10.
18. The Minister-President of Rhineland-Palatinate, Bernhard Vogel, gave a clear viewpoint on this during his talk to the *Deutsche Gesellschaft für Außenpolitik* on 19 February 1987, entitled 'Gibt es eine Außenpolitik der Länder? Eine Klarstellung aus der Sicht eines Ministerpräsidenten'. The transcription of this talk was published by the *Gesellschaft*.
19. The description originates from Ottokar Hahn, Minister for Federal and European affairs in the Saarland in his 'EG-Engagement der Länder: Lobbyismus oder Nebenaußenpolitik?, in Hrbek and Thaysen, op. cit., 109.
20. Rudolf W. Strohmeier, 'Möglichkeiten der Einflußnahme auf den Entscheidungsprozeß der Europäischen Gemeinschaften durch die deutschen Bundesländer nach Einrichtung von Länderbüros in Brüssel', *Die Öffentliche Verwaltung* (1988), 633–7.
21. This confirms once again the governmental and administrative nature of German federalism.
22. See Rudolf Hrbek, 'Bundesländer und Regionalismus in der EG' in Magiera and Merten (1988), 127–49, and Georg-Berndt Oschatz, 'Normsetzung der Länder in einem Europa der Regionen: Gesetzgebung oder Satzungserlaß?' *Zeischrift für Gesetzgebung* (1990), 14–23.
23. During its session of 16 February 1990, the *Bundesrat* passed a resolution on the 'Community Charter of Regionalisation' of the European Parliament (*Bundesrats-Drucksache* 279/89. Beschluß). One of the points in this resolution was as follows: 'In the view of the *Bundesrat*, comprehensive and effective regionalisation within the EC is an important precondition for the political weight of regions in the Community to be strengthened and for steps towards integration to be in line with the principles of a federal system'. The representatives of the *Länder* also repeat their established views on the principle of subsidiarity and on the role of the *Länder* in the European Community in this resolution.
24. The *Länder* of Bavaria, Hesse, North-Rhine-Westphalia and Rhineland-Palatinate proposed this motion; see *Bundesrats-Drucksache* 703/89.
25. See *Bundestags-Drucksache* 11/7391.

6 Efficiency, democracy and West German federalism: a critical analysis

Simon Bulmer

Introduction

This chapter is designed to raise some of the wider issues concerning the development, functioning and purposes of West German federalism. It aims to present a critical analysis from a British perspective and examine 'costs' and 'benefits' of the federal order.[1]

All systems of government are seen as facing a dilemma between efficiency in the provision of governmental services, implying 'big' government, and local democratic accountability, which implies 'small' government. The West German political system is no exception in this regard. As a federal system it should be well placed to benefit from the positive compromise between efficiency and democracy that federalism is supposed to facilitate.

Thus West German federalism should ensure such efficiency goals as sound performance of the economy and responsiveness to international developments or to technological change. It should also secure relatively uniform social and welfare provision: a task formally set down in Articles 72 (2/3) and 106 (3) of the Basic Law. The goals of efficiency do not automatically translate into a process of centralisation, for this might over-burden the federal level. However, in West Germany such a centralisation process has occurred. This situation has been compounded by the Basic Law authorising the Federal Republic to 'transfer sovereign powers to intergovernmental institutions' (Article 24), thus potentially involving a supranational level of policy provision. As will be argued, it is the formal setting-up of these efficiency goals which has had a creeping, but significant impact upon West German federalism. In fact it can be considered to endorse Nevil Johnson's comment that 'the demand for regular, equal and extensive provision of services tends to establish institutional behaviour patterns which come into conflict with the traditional postulates of democratic government'.[2]

The West German federal system was, of course, created with a view to assuring democratic government. It was but one of several pieces of constitutional engineering undertaken to this end. However, this was in large measure a reflection of the Western allies' concerns about a further centralising regime of the nature of the Third Reich. To be sure, there was a German tradition of federalism and there were indeed some strong internal pressures for federalism in the post-war period. The fact is, however, that the main driving force for West German federalism did not derive from the need to secure the democratic rights of geographically concentrated, national, linguistic, cultural or ethnic minorities. Whilst it would be a dangerous exaggeration to regard West German society as homogeneous in nature, it is important to remember that the underpinning for federalism is relatively weak in terms of societal cleavages. Hence it could be argued that the principles of federalism have been upheld more by means of constitutional judgements and by the assertiveness of *Länder* governments than by diverse societal interests.[3]

So, if West German federalism does not mirror societal diversity, due to the special circumstances of its origins, does it act as a guarantee for accountability? In judging performance on this criterion it will be necessary to question how far there is a clear delineation between the powers of the federation and those of the *Länder*, for clear lines of responsibility are an important requirement for democratic accountability.

In this chapter I will present three arguments relating to efficiency, democracy and West German federalism. Firstly, I will argue that West Germany has placed efficiency ahead of (local) democratic accountability. Second, I will argue that this has occurred because of the way that federalism is institutionalised in West Germany. Thirdly, I will question whether German federalism does successfully promote 'efficiency' as defined above.

Centralisation and efficiency

One of the key features of West German federalism is the principle of subsidiarity, embodied in several articles of the Basic Law (Articles 30, 70 and 83), which hold that political problems should be solved locally in so far as this is possible. The West German federal system thus set out from a situation of *Länder* predominance. However, as is well known, this predominance has not continued because of the process of centralisation that has taken place. The gradual transfer of policy responsibilities from the *Länder* to the *Bund* has taken two forms. There have been

changes to the Basic Law itself; between 1949 and 1984, twenty-four of
the thirty-five laws amending the constitution had an impact on the
federal order.[4] Secondly, the *Länder* have become increasingly dependent upon the *Bund* in financial terms. The latter development has
either prompted some of the above-mentioned constitutional changes or
has engendered a less formal financial dependency on the *Bund*. The
process of centralisation has been a pronounced one, although there has
been some limited compensation in the generous interpretation given to
'*Zustimmungsbedürftigkeit*'; whether the Bundesrat's consent is required
for legislation.[5] In addition, there have been policy areas where *Länder*
governments have successfully resisted the transfer of power through
resort to the Federal Constitutional Court, the 'arbiter of the federal
system'.[6]

Constitutional transfers of authority

It is worth giving some detailed attention to both forms which centralisation has taken. First, then, what can be said about the constitutional
transfers of authority? Commentators have generally identified two
periods of centralisation, to which we can now add a third.[7] In the 1950s
the *Bund* experienced a relative increase in its power, although not
exclusively at the expense of the *Länder*. This was because the ending of
the allies' occupation statute resulted in the Federal Republic acquiring
responsibility for foreign and defence policies. These powers had never
been *Länder* powers and it would have been a bizarre interpretation of
the subsidiarity principle to have suggested that these policy areas
should be other than the responsibility of the *Bund*. Apart from these
special circumstances, there were also a number of new issues coming on
to the political agenda where exclusive *Länder* responsibility was deemed
inappropriate to efficient policy delivery. Thus civil aviation became an
exclusive *Bund* responsibility, whilst 'the production and utilisation of
nuclear energy' became a concurrent power. In both these instances
deviation from the principle of subsidiarity can be seen as a triumph for
'efficiency'.

The second period of centralisation came with the economic and
financial reforms of 1967–9. It was during this period, when the existence of the Grand Coalition in Bonn facilitated a reassessment of the
federal system in a climate of party political consensus, that major
changes were agreed. The *Bund* obtained significant new economic
policy powers designed to enable Keynesian macroeconomic management. In fact such macroeconomic management proved to be virtually
unworkable, due to problems of political coordination, and subsequently

became less fashionable as well. Nonetheless, the principle was established that the *Bund* could seek to influence the budgetary policy-making of the *Länder* on the basis of macroeconomic considerations. Far-reaching decisions for the shape of federalism also resulted from the financial reform (on which, see below). Again a number of constitutional amendments were agreed with a view to ensuring a more efficient provision of services. For example, several policies – regional policy, agricultural structural policy and higher education construction – were deemed matters which the *Länder* alone could provide for neither financially nor without jeopardising the improvement of living conditions for society as a whole (the commitment in Article 72 (3)). Hence the result was a further weakening of *Länder* autonomy, with goals of efficiency explicitly invoked by legislators.

We have arguably experienced – or are experiencing – a third period of centralisation in the mid-/late-1980s. Of importance to this has been the European Community's Single European Act. The *Länder* have consistently been supporters of European integration but, right from the establishment of the European Coal and Steel Community in 1952, there has been an impact upon the federal order.[8] The *Länder* took the opportunity presented by the need for *Bundesrat* ratification of the Rome Treaties to request the creation of a constitution procedure. Known as the Article 2 procedure, this was designed to ensure that the *Länder* were consulted on such EC policy items that, ordinarily, would have been their own business under the principle of subsidiarity. The creation of the post of *Länder* Observer, responsible for monitoring those activities of the EC which impinged upon *Länder* responsibilities as defined in the Basic Law, was a further device aimed at limiting the centralising effects of European integration on German federalism. These arrangements proved to function reasonably successfully but from the late 1970s problems began to arise relating to the EC's incipient legislation on environmental policy, an area not explicitly covered in the EC treaties themselves but one of the key remaining areas where the *Länder* retained predominant responsibility.

This grievance between the *Länder* and the *Bund* came to a head with the agreement amongst EC foreign ministers in February 1986 on the Single European Act (SEA). The SEA represented the first comprehensive revision of the EC treaties and, amongst other things, provided the constitutional–legal basis for EC environmental policy. The fact that the West German Foreign Office (i.e. the *Bund*) had conducted the EC-level bargaining – which the *Länder* regarded as 'negotiating away' important parts of their constitutional authority – raised the political stakes in the matter. Despite the opposition of the *Länder* governments as a whole, and particularly those with Social-Democrat-led governments and Bavaria, the *Länder* pulled back from refusing to ratify the SEA: a step which would have scuppered a crucial development for European integration as a whole. Instead a new procedure for *Bund–Länder* coordination on European policy was negotiated. When the EC discusses policy areas where the *Länder* have constitutional authority within the FRG, the procedure allows for *Bund–Länder* negotiations in advance with a view to reaching an agreed position. A *Länder* representative may be permitted to be a member of the federal government's delegation at meetings of the Council of Ministers or of intergovernmental committees. However, all such involvement by the *Länder* is indirect lobbying; it is subject to the agreement of Bonn. Direct lobbying of the Commission by the *Länder* would be regarded as a challenge to the federal government's exclusive responsibility for foreign policy.

Hence the SEA has had a centralising effect and in two ways. First, as illustrated by the case of environmental policy, increased federal involvement has been introduced and given a constitutional basis, since the *Bund* represents German interests within the intergovernmental institutions of the EC. If the federal government needs to, it can invoke 'integration policy' to justify its deviation from the negotiating position sought by the *Länder* governments. Given that EC policy-making is all about package-dealing, it will be against German interests to be inflexible due to *Länder* wishes. This situation applies not only to the environment but also to research policy, for instance. Second, the commitment to completion of the internal market, for which the EC was constitutionally empowered by the Rome Treaties, will have an impact. For example, constraints on public tendering by *Länder* agencies will become actual rather than potential, with agreement on public procurement rules. A further point should be made in this context. The commitment to increased use of majority voting in the EC Council of Ministers will present problems where the *Länder* attempt to bind the federal government to a negotiating position to be presented in Brussels. The federal government may simply be outvoted. Among the policy areas of importance to the *Länder* that will be affected in some way by the SEA are: education and culture, broadcasting, regional policy, agricultural structural policy, consumer protection, some financial services regulation and research policy. The organisation of local government and policing are the only exclusive *Länder* competences which appear to be 'spared', but there may even be encroachment on the latter.

It must be remembered that, in addition to the SEA, there have been other forces at work that have promoted centralisation. The Chernobyl nuclear accident brought into focus the problems of having dispersed authority for matters of public safety and led to the creation in June 1986 of the Federal Ministry for Environmental Affairs. Public concern about this accident and a series of chemical spillages into the Rhine was clearly supportive of some centralisation of policy responsibility.[9]

Financial centralisation[10]

Closely related to the formal constitutional transfers of authority out-lined above there has been a creeping centralisation in federal finances. Already in 1955 the system of apportioning tax revenue had been amended in favour of the *Bund*. The 1969 financial reform was largely motivated by the need to enable the *Länder* to cope with the increasing expenditure burden of carrying out their constitutional duties. The financially weaker *Länder* experienced budgetary problems, necessitat-ing changes to the principles of financial equalisation in order that the Basic Law's commitment to federation-wide uniformity of living stan-dards should not be breached. The broad outcome of this challenge to the finances of federalism has been an increased use of mixed *Bund–Länder* financing of individual projects and of federal subsidies to the *Länder*. Hence the original attempt of the Basic Law to provide separate revenue sources for the *Bund* and the *Länder* has not worked out.

Although the formal position is that the federal government should not interfere with the budgetary autonomy of the *Länder* governments, as set down in Article 109 (1) of the Basic Law, the autonomy of the latter has been compromised. The picture, therefore, is one of close financial interdependence such that *Länder* governments have to con-sider very carefully the economics of investment projects which fail to meet the criteria for grants-in-aid from the federal government.[11] The reallocation of federal power which also occurred at the time of the Grand Coalition provided for even further interdependence between the *Länder* and the *Bund*, notably through the establishment of the joint tasks with their mixed funding arrangements.

Moving forward to more recent times, the finances of federalism have been upset by the economic changes associated with the oil crises and the information technology revolution. The blows suffered by some of the northern *Länder* due to their dependence on the 'old' industries – coal, steel and shipbuilding – has led to the creation of new economic bur-dens. Individual states have had to respond to social problems while needing to increase their investment programmes to attract new industry. This is obviously not possible if the state is suffering from stagnating, or declining, tax revenue. For a city-state such as Bremen, with its reliance on older industry, the problems are profound. If it were to seek to increase its tax revenue, it might simply prompt company relocation beyond the city limits to Lower Saxony, thus worsening the situation still further.

The result of this problem has been twofold. Firstly, it culminated in the (then) five SPD-governed *Länder* and Baden-Württemberg chal-lenging the horizontal equalisation system before the Federal

Constitutional Court.[12] The Court's June 1986 ruling declared that much of the system was contrary to the constitution and it also ruled that there should be changes to the vertical equalisation system between the *Bund* and the *Länder*.[13] Secondly, and against the background of renegotiating the financial equalisation systems, there resulted a period of extensive pressure being exerted by the northern *Länder* for more aid from Bonn. During 1988 the governments of the Saarland and of North-Rhine-Westphalia pressed for a special programme of aid for the depressed coal and steel areas.[14] But it was bolstered by a more broadly based coalition of northern German interests, the '*Konferenz Norddeutschland*', which sought an increased federal contribution to (their) social welfare payments. The Christian Democratic Minister-President of Lower Saxony, Ernst Albrecht, was prominent in these cross-party demands.

The eventual outcome of these demands was in fact a structural aid package ('*Strukturhilfegesetz*') of DM 2,450 million per annum, from which only Hesse and Baden-Württemberg would not be beneficiaries.[15] Lothar Späth, the Minister-President of Baden-Württemberg, immediately announced his intention to challenge the legality of this before the Federal Constitutional Court, not because his state was to receive no benefits but because, in his view, the aid merely represented an additional form of financial equalisation rather than a properly targeted system of structural aid. The whole financing of federalism has thus become highly complex with the *Länder* becoming increasingly reliant on the *Bund*. To this development we must add the emergent EC involvement in *Länder* finances. This will add a major constraint if indirect tax approximation is agreed (as proposed in the single market programme).

In terms both of the transfer of constitutional responsibilities and of the shift in financial power, West German federalism has been characterised by a process of centralisation. The commitment to uniformity of living standards has been behind many of the changes which have been made. The Federal Republic's commitment to European integration has similarly increased the tendencies toward centralisation. It would perhaps be unwise to present the EC as an efficient 'supplier' of policy, given the mixed record of the Common Agricultural Policy. Nevertheless, the whole basis of the SEA was a recognition that in certain policy areas the EC level needed to be harnessed to national systems, particularly in a climate of 'global regionalism' in the Western economies, to assure continued prosperity and welfare. But if such centralisation has stemmed primarily from the needs of efficiency, what happened to democratic accountability?

Centralisation and democratic accountability

Apart from the institutional checks upon centralisation – namely the Federal Constitutional Court and the *Bundesrat* – the real reservoir of support for federalism should surely be the voters in the *Länder*. What has been their role in this centralisation process? A fully documented answer to this question cannot be offered here but some hypotheses are suggested.

First of all, there does not seem to have been much popular opposition to the centralisation process itself. It would appear that the electorate is more concerned with the political system's efficiency at providing relative uniformity of living conditions, at ensuring continued economic growth, and at protecting the environment. For example, in a survey conducted in October 1989, 86 per cent of West German respondents stated their preference for laws regarding pollution being decided by the EC as a whole rather than by each member state individually (8 per cent).[16] On this issue the supranational level has supplanted the federation which itself only gained powers through constitutional changes. On policing matters, public opinion has not been tolerant of the uncoordinated pursuit of criminals, never mind terrorists, and was supportive of the establishment under 1973 legislation of the Federal Criminal Office and of the creation of GSG 9, the anti-terrorist unit organised within the Federal Border Guard. The policing issue was thrown into relief in September 1988 with the rather uncoordinated and uneven response of different *Länder* police forces to a kidnapping in northern Germany. The situation was hardly improved by the Bavarian police force – which was uninvolved – mounting a demonstration of how it would have solved the crisis!

Second, and arguably underlying the first hypothesis, is West Germany's relative social homogeneity. Livingston alerted analysts to the societal dimension of federalism.[17] Following his perspective, might it not be argued that the absence of popular opposition to the creeping centralisation has also resulted from the artificial nature of German federalism? Which are the social groups that would defend the autonomy of an individual *Land* against the process of centralisation? Little real attention was given to social divisions in the creation of the German federal system. Perhaps only religion was relevant in this connection but the *Länder* boundaries do not correlate to concentrations of religious denomination. Moreover, many of the *Länder* themselves are artificial creations geographically. With one or two exceptions, notably Bavaria, there is little *Länder* 'patriotism', although the federal system as a whole enjoys support. Bavaria is a special case because, with the prominence of 'its own' political party – the Christian Social Union – it has a *political* organisation (as opposed to a social group) which can defend the *Land*'s autonomy. Overall, then, it is argued that public opinion has tended to favour the predominance of 'efficiency' over 'democracy' in the evolution of federalism. The reason for this lies primarily with the origins of the Federal Republic itself.

Third, the Federal Republic has been a consistent supporter of European integration. Although levels of support in public opinion have declined somewhat in recent years, there is a continuing recognition of West Germany's need for continued good relations with trading partners in Western Europe. The imperatives of the 1950s may no longer exist in this regard but the alternatives remained until recently very limited due to the unresolved German question.[18]

These three hypotheses are advanced as explaining why the forces pushing for 'efficiency' were chiefly resisted for reasons for self-interest by *Länder* politicians using the Federal Constitutional Court and the *Bundesrat* rather than by more broadly based opposition. How far does the federal system act as a guarantor of local democratic accountability?

In addressing this question I will adopt a critical approach. The term usually invoked to characterise West German federalism is 'cooperative federalism'. This was to be the leitmotiv of *Bund–Länder* relations following the reforms of the Grand Coalition. Cooperative federalism sought to justify federalism at a time of increasing centralisation by emphasising the predominance of those policy areas where the *Bund* and the *Länder* act in harness rather than autonomously of each other. The danger of such a system, whether in the Federal Republic or, for that matter, in the EC, lies in the risk that intergovernmental relations predominate. In other words, there is the danger that policy is made between governments of the *Bund* and the *Länder*, or between their civil servants, in such a manner as to limit accountability. Is the plethora of such committees established in order to run West German federalism a guarantee for local democratic accountability? Or could such accountability be assured just as well in a unitary system of government? Is it possible to identify the channels of political accountability? Doubts must be expressed on all these counts.

West German intergovernmental relations exist on four levels. Several hundred *Länder–Länder* committees exist in those policy areas where the states hold exclusive authority (whether on the making or implementation of policy, or on the associated legal processes). Even greater numbers of such committees exist at the *Bund–Länder* level. The joint tasks involve a special pattern of *Bund–Länder* relations but raise similar questions of local accountability. Finally, there is the increasing emergence of areas where *Bund–Länder* relations have the EC level grafted on top, thus making the network of intergovernmental contacts still more impenetrable. Attempts to find integrated policies and actions in these various areas (through '*Politikverflechtung*') has inevitably increased the bureaucratisation of policy-making. Democracy has been seriously weakened since the *Länder* parliaments have lost much of their power. Having power where competences are shared with other government levels is, in my opinion, a poor substitute.

West Germany's federal system has clearly placed greater emphasis upon the provision of 'efficiency' rather than upon assuring democratic accountability. I have argued that the evolving West German policy agenda has alighted upon a succession of issues where the *Länder* held responsibility. Be it concerns about a potential scientific and educational gap (the '*Bildungskatastrophe*' debate in the 1960s), fears of economic recession in the mid-1960s, or concern about environmental protection, the general picture has been fairly similar. The *Bund* – and in some cases the EC – has had to be brought in (or in the latter case has come in at the federal government's invitation) whether to provide a coordinated policy or to provide the financial wherewithal. Why has this occurred?

Creeping centralisation: a neo-institutional perspective[19]

One way of looking at creeping centralisation is in the terms of neo-institutional analysis. This approach takes a broader view of institutions than has been the case traditionally. Hall regards institutions as referring to 'the formal rules, compliance procedures, and standard operating practices that structure the relationship between individuals in various units of the polity and economy'.[20] The argument is that institutions thus defined introduce their own dynamics into state–society relations. What is new here is the extension of institutions beyond the organisation of the state apparatus to include the organisation of finance and industry, of the labour market, the country's position in the international economy and the political system as a whole.[21]

Looking first of all at the state apparatus, it is clear that there is a tension between the formal commitment in the Basic Law to uniformity of living conditions, on the one hand, and the assumptions of the subsidiarity principle, on the other. This tension has been reflected in many of the cases brought before the Federal Constitutional Court. However, important though this institution has been, Philip Blair has pointed out, with reference to the period from the 1960s, that 'increasingly it would appear that major developments in the federal system have passed the Court by'.[22] He is referring to the developments which took place under the heading of cooperative federalism following the Report of the Troeger Commission, established by federal and *Länder* governments. Cooperative federalism was specifically advanced in the report because of the need of the federal order to adapt to changing political, economic and social conditions.[23] So, while the Court has remained an important guarantor of *Länder* power, the growth of cooperative federalism has resulted in important shifts of authority, in some important cases beyond the Court's 'reach'.

The tension between the constitutional commitment to the transfer of power to intergovernmental institutions (Article 24, Basic Law) and the principle of subsidiarity is also relevant. Transfer of *Länder* powers to the EC has not been challenged before the Federal Constitutional Court. A major reason for this has been the broad consensus in public opinion, the parties and the *Länder* favouring European integration. The closest to such a challenge came when the Bavarian state government took its counterpart in Bonn to the Federal Constitutional Court alleging that *Länder* interests had been insufficiently taken into account during negotiations on the EC's broadcasting directive.[24] The federal government had conducted these negotiations on behalf of the *Länder*, which are exclusively competent for broadcasting matters. The Bavarian government's case was rejected by the Court. The whole question of where the dividing line exists in the EC's activities between foreign policy (the *Bund*'s competence) and more specialist policy areas (with various configurations of competence) still remains uncharted territory.

Thus the resolution to both tensions has been institutionalised in an array of policy-making bodies. Further, it has been underpinned by the generous interpretation of the *Bundesrat*'s legislative power. That this resolution has occurred can be seen in terms of the institutional dynamics of the political system. The quiescence of West German public opinion and inter-party consensus on the creation of cooperative federalism have prevailed. Given the constitutional guarantees with regard to the assignment of powers, it is clear that public opinion or party forces could have obstructed these processes of centralisation. The absence of regionally concentrated social diversity has already been remarked upon.

If we identify cooperative federalism and European integration as important causes of centralisation, then it is important to look beneath them for deeper explanations. First, it is important to recognise the way West Germany is anchored institutionally into the international system. European integration and acceptance in the Western world as objectives of German policy pre-date restoration of sovereignty in foreign and defence policy. Moreover the Federal Republic is firmly committed to a global system of free trade. This is reflected in EC membership but is underpinned domestically by an array of institutions and attitudes associated with the social market economy. Given these commitments and the FRG's resultant dependence on foreign trade, it is incumbent on the political system that it adapts to changing international circumstances. This situation is further reinforced by the institutions of industry, finance and labour, all three of which share a fundamental commitment to liberal trade and the social market economy, with all this entails.

As a result of these broader institutional factors, then, it is clear that the goal of 'efficiency' has enjoyed much wider institutionalised support than the goal of local democratic accountability within, in most cases, artificially created *Länder*.

Federalism and efficiency

I have argued that the centralisation of West German federalism can be explained in terms of the priority accorded to 'efficiency' over 'local democracy'. However, it should not be assumed that West German federalism is a passport to efficient public policy. Fritz Scharpf has identified the obstacles which the FRG's system of cooperative federalism can bring to policy-making.[25] As well as identifying the decline in democratic accountability brought about by the bureaucratisation of *Bund–Länder* relations, he has also identified the 'joint-decision trap'. This trap, Scharpf argues, derives from the tendency to prefer unanimous decisions within cooperative federalist bodies. How does this trap come about?

In the case of the joint tasks Scharpf presents evidence that, despite the provision for majority voting within the relevant *Bund–Länder* committees, this is not always practised. '*Länder* solidarity . . . prevented the federal government from playing the interests of some *Länder* against others in order to form the "minimum winning coalitions".'[26] In concrete terms he sees this preference for solidarity (i.e. the joint-decision trap) as explaining a number of less than satisfactory policy outcomes. Agricultural structural policy is argued to favour the northern *Länder* rather than the southern states where agricultural inefficiency is more of a problem.[27] Similarly, the regional policy joint task has not proved flexible enough to tackle the particular problems of geographically concentrated industrial decline, e.g. of the steel industry in the Saar or of shipbuilding in Bremen.[28] As a result special programmes have had to be developed and these have tended to undermine the policy rationality which the joint tasks were to provide. In both cases the joint-decision trap is presented as an explanation for suboptimal policy.

This kind of problem is in no way restricted to joint tasks, however. For example the *Bund*'s exclusive competence for major (federal) highways is in fact constrained by dependence on the *Länder* for providing information on policy needs and for implementation.[29] Hence there may be brakes upon policy responsiveness even in areas of exclusive federal competence. Other analysis has suggested that the dynamics and procedures of the *Bund–Länder* joint programme in hospital construction have contributed to excess capacity in hospital provision.[30] Other examples exist where cooperative federalism may have hampered policy outcomes.[31] These include counter-cyclical policy under the Stability and Growth Act, reform of the West German stock exchanges until 1989–90, and industrial policy.[32]

The last of these policy areas deserves some especial mention. Reference has already been made to the problems encountered in targetting areas of industrial decline in the regional policy joint task. This has encouraged the use of special programmes as well as independent *Länder* initiatives. The policies of Baden-Württemberg have been particularly publicised. Under the influence of CDU Minister-President Lothar Späth, a quite comprehensive programme of interventionist policies has been developed: training policy, financial aid to facilitate the development plans of small- and medium-sized enterprises, a programme of promoting high technology and even a system of export guarantee credits.[33]

This is symptomatic of a proliferation of *Länder* policies designed to attract inward investment against the backdrop of an emergent South–North divide in the FRG. With the policies being developed in the individual *Länder* this strikes a blow in favour of local accountability and against the bureaucratisation of cooperative federalism and '*Politikverflechtung*'. However, questions have begun to be raised regarding the needless duplication in policy, of too many investment opportunities chasing too few investments.[34] It is instructive that in October 1986 the European Commission instituted proceedings against the Baden-Württemberg government under Article 93 of the EEC Treaty, accusing it of unfair state aid in connection with a proposed Daimler-Benz plant in Rastatt.[35] If the Commission finds this a potential threat at the EC level, there must surely be distortion within the Federal Republic itself. How does such '*Kleinstaaterei*' square with the principles of uniformity of living conditions and equalisation of *Länder* finances?

Clearly it is not possible to review the performance of the federal system across the whole spectrum of public policy provision. And I have played up the economic policy area in particular, whereas others could point to cases of the *Länder* acting as factors of stability in a period of upheaval. For example, it could be argued that the federal system has served to defend public sector broadcasting from over-hasty deregulation because of the need to reach inter-party (and inter-*Land*) agreement in the face of the transnational challenge of satellite broadcasting. It could also be argued that wide access to higher education (with reasonably comparable opportunities between regions of the FRG) has been assured in the context of the needs after 1992.[36] More broadly, the inevitable need in West Germany's federal system to reach agreement between governments of different shadings has the effect of virtually eliminating the more dramatic, and potentially damaging, policy changes associated with unitary states such as Britain. These examples, just as those cited earlier concerning suboptimal policy outcomes, involve delicate value judgments about efficiency and about the most appropriate form of policy. But such issues must be assessed in any analysis of forty years of West German federalism.

Conclusion

Over the past forty years the West German federal system has undergone significant changes which have shifted the *Bund–Länder* balance considerably. I have suggested in this chapter that centralisation has been a product of the wish to provide adequate public policy in a country which is exposed to international competition, technological change and is committed to European integration. Also important has been the lack of resistance to this centralisation on the part of the electorate. However, the particular line of development that has been followed, namely cooperative federalism, does involve a complex interdependency between the *Bund* and the *Länder* governments (plus the EC). At best it is a factor promoting stability; at worst it creates immobilism.

It is striking that, with the 1982 change of government, Chancellor Kohl sought a change of policy precisely towards granting the *Länder* more autonomy (*'Entflechtung'*).[37] This attempt at disengagement, however, has raised new questions about uniformity of living standards as some of the southern *Länder* have enjoyed more dynamic economies and, in consequence, greater financial freedom to attract further inward investment. The competitiveness has even extended to the EC, since all the *Länder* governments had by May 1988 established information bureaux in Brussels. Hamburg, Lower Saxony and Schleswig-Holstein share the services of Herr Haferkamp, the former EC commissioner, which indicates the importance attached to the office. The stakes in securing balanced economic growth are very high. They have been raised further by the need for all *Länder* to respond to the challenges of completion of the EC's internal market. Whether German interests are best served by attempts at *'Entflechtung'*, at a time when the European context has become especially important, remains to be seen. Similarly, the challenges to the finances of federalism are bound to be particularly pronounced in the future.

I have argued that the development of the federal system has raised some obstacles to democratic accountability. However, two remarks need to be made in this connection. First, democracy itself can be defined in different ways. Clear lines of accountability are most closely associated with the Westminster model of democracy. They are less associated with the alternative, consensus model of democracy, in which inclusive and consensual patterns of negotiation predominate over adversarial and oppositional forms.[38] West German federalism has become a prominent example of this consensus model. Secondly, we must remind ourselves of the purposes of the creation of West German federalism. For the Western allies, and especially the United States and France, the objective was to prevent the recurrence of a centralising regime along the lines of the Third Reich. In assuring democratic rule in this sense, West German federalism has been an unqualified success. And it offers the most attractive framework for the reunification of the two Germanies following the dramatic developments in the second half of 1989.

Notes

1. This is a revised version of a paper given at the conference organised by the Centre for Federal Studies, University of Leicester, in September 1989 on 'Forty Years of West German Federalism'. I am grateful for comments made by participants at the conference. Some of the issues discussed in this chapter are also considered from a different perspective in S. Bulmer, 'Territorial government', in G. Smith, W.E. Paterson and P.H. Merkl (eds), *Developments in West German politics*, Macmillan, London (1989).
2. N. Johnson, 'Some effects of decentralisation in the Federal Republic of Germany', in L.J. Sharpe (ed.), *Decentralist trends in Western Democracies*, Sage, London (1979), 235–58. The trade-off between efficiency and democracy is not an immediate one: see G. Smith, *Politics in Western Europe*, 5th ed, Gower, Aldershot (1989), 257. In addition, the assumption that big government equates with efficient government is itself the subject of much debate.
3. See Philip Blair's contribution to this volume.
4. H. Laufer, *Der Föderalismus in der Bundesrepublik Deutschland*, Informationen zur politischen Bildung no. 204, Bundeszentrale für politische Bildung, Bonn (1976), 12.
5. Instead of some 10 per cent of legislation requiring *Bundesrat* consent, as was anticipated originally, the figure now exceeds 50 per cent. This practice was largely confirmed by the Constitutional Court in 1974.
6. See P. Blair, *Federalism and judicial review in West Germany*, Clarendon Press, Oxford (1981), 9.
7. See, for instance, H. Klatt, 'Reform und Perspektiven des Föderalismus in der Bundesrepublik Deutschland', *Aus Politik und Zeitgeschichte*, 12 July 1986, 3–21.
8. S. Bulmer, *The domestic structure of European Community policy-making in West Germany*, Garland Inc., New York (1986), Chs 5–6; S. Bulmer and W. Paterson, *The Federal Republic of Germany and the European Community*,

Allen & Unwin, London (1987), Ch. 8; R. Hrbek and U. Thaysen (eds), *Die deutschen Länder und die Europäischen Gemeinschaften*, Nomos Verlagsgesellschaft, Baden-Baden (1986). See also Rudolf Hrbek's contribution to this volume.

9. In fact the domestic transfer of constitutional authority relating to legislation on the environment was under way in the early 1970s. Refuse disposal, clean air and noise abatement were added to the catalogue of concurrent powers in 1972 (under Article 74 (24) of the Basic Law), thus gi ng the *Bund* new powers.

10. For an English language account of the finances of federalism, see J. Knott, *Managing the German economy: budgetary politics in a federal state*, D.C. Heath, Lexington, Mass. (1981).

11. This kind of situation is not exclusive to federal political systems, for it can also be seen in local authority budgeting in the United Kingdom. Local authorities are likely to be influenced in their prioritising of investment projects where the EC potentially offers financial support from its regional fund.

12. Under the system of horizontal equalisation, North-Rhine-Westphalia, Baden-Württemberg, Hesse and Hamburg have been the contributors, while Bavaria, Lower Saxony, Rhineland-Palatinate, Bremen and the Saar have been the recipients. The court case was brought by a mixture of contributing and recipient *Länder* sharing the conviction that the system was unfair.

13. O.-E. Geske, 'Konturen eines neuen Länderfinanzausgleichs', *Wirtschaftsdienst*, **66** (1988), 399–403.

14. 'Rau will viel Geld von Bonn sehen', *Frankfurter Allgemeine Zeitung*, 19 February 1988, 12.

15. *Frankfurter Allgemeine Zeitung*, 17 December 1988.

16. Survey conducted by Harris Research Centre and European Associates for *The Independent*, Channel Four, *Süddeutsche Zeitung*, *El Páis* and *Le Monde*. See *The Independent*, 18 November 1989, 7.

17. W. Livingston, 'A note on the nature of federalism', *Political Science Quarterly*, **67** (1952), 81–95.

18. See Chapter 9 of this volume.

19. It is not possible within the confines of this chapter to give a complete exposition of neo-institutional analysis. I am following the broad approach of Peter Hall. See P. Hall, *Governing the economy: the politics of state intervention in Britain and France*, Polity Press, Oxford (1986). For a neo-institutional analysis of the West German policy process, see S. Bulmer, 'Unity, diversity and stability: the "efficient secrets" of West German public policy?', in S. Bulmer (ed.), *The changing agenda of West German public policy*, Dartmouth, Aldershot (1989), 13–39.

20. Hall (1986), 19.

21. ibid., 29–34.

22. Blair (1981), 207.

23. ibid., 209.

24. The Bavarian Government's case was rejected by the Federal Constitutional Court.

25. F. Scharpf, *Politischer Immobilismus und ökonomische Krise – Aufsätze zu den politischen Restriktionen der Wirtschaftspolitik in der Bundesrepublik Deutschland*, Athenäum, Kronberg (1977); F. Scharpf, 'The joint-decision trap: lessons from German federalism and European integration'. Discussion Paper IIM/LMP 85–1, Wissenschaftszentrum, Berlin (1985); F. Scharpf *et al.*, *Politikverflechtung: Theorie und Empirie des kooperativen Föderalismus in der Bundesrepublik*, Scriptor, Kronberg (1977).

26. Scharpf (1985), 11–12.

27. ibid., 13–14.

28. ibid., 14–15.

29. D. Garlichs and C. Hull, 'Central control and information dependence', in K. Hanf and F. Scharpf (eds), *Interorganisational policymaking: limits to coordination and central control*, Sage, London (1978).

30. Research by Schnabel, reported by Scharpf (1985), 13.

31. S. Bulmer and P. Humphreys, 'Kohl, Corporatism and Congruence: the West German model under challenge', in Bulmer (1989), 177–97.

32. See respectively Knott (1981); M. Moran, 'A state of inaction: the state and stock exchange reform in the FRG', in Bulmer (1989), 110–27; R. Sturm, 'The industrial policy debate in the FRG', in Bulmer (1989), 155–74.

33. R. Schoeck, 'Methoden und Ergebnisse finanzieller Wirtschaftsförderung', in R. Henn (ed.), *Technologie, Wachstum und Beschäftigung: Festschrift für Lothar Späth*, Springer Verlag, Berlin (1987), 685–96.

34. For an overview, see R. Sturm, 'The industrial policy debate in the FRG', in Bulmer (1989).

35. P. Klemmer, 'Die Kontroverse um die Daimler-Benz Beihilfe', *Wirtschaftsdienst*, **66** (1986), 550–4.

36. A review of the balance between efficiency and equality/stability is provided in S. Bulmer and P. Humphreys, 'Kohl, corporatism and congruence: the West German model under challenge', in Bulmer (1989).

37. Klatt (1986). See also Hartmut Klatt's contribution to this volume.

38. A. Lijphart, *Democracies: patterns of majoritarian and consensus government in twenty-one countries*, Yale University Press, New Haven (1984).

7 Centralising trends in the Federal Republic: the record of the Kohl Chancellorship

Hartmut Klatt

The federal structure of West Germany did not emerge through the union of a series of previously independent states, but as a result of the re-emergence of political structures on a regional, or *Land* level within the Western Occupation Zones of post-war Germany (a process supported and encouraged by the Western occupying powers). Ethnic, religious and linguistic divisions did not play a role. Nevertheless, the ten *Länder* (eleven if we include West Berlin, which has a different legal status) are certainly different in terms of size, population, geography and economic and social structure. However, in spite of these regional differences, there are unmistakable trends towards a harmonisation of living conditions across the different *Länder* and towards a concentration of political–administrative decision-making at the central level. In political and academic discussions, these developments have been analysed through the employment of such concepts as the 'unitary federal state', 'cooperative federalism' or 'intergovernmental relations' (*'Politikverflechtung'*). This chapter will examine this process of centralisation and harmonisation throughout the history of the Federal Republic and will present an assessment of the current situation which has emerged under the Chancellorship of Helmut Kohl.[1]

The origins and initial stages of development of West German federalism

The situation in 1949

The Basic Law of 1949 was dominated by the principle of a functional division of responsibilities between the federation and *Länder*: legislative powers, administrative authority, responsibility for the adjudication of conflicts and for public financing were divided and shared between the federal and *Länder* governments. Moreover, a limited number of functional areas in legislation, administration and finance were given to the federal or *Länder* governments separately. The Basic Law thus provides for a relatively strict division of powers in which the designated organs of both levels of government were intended to perform their functions autonomously and on their own responsibility. In the area of finance, there was a further division of responsibility in which the federal and *Länder* governments were, in principle, to finance their own particular functions. Tax revenues were thus assigned separately either to the federal or to the *Länder* governments.

However, on the other hand, the system of divided powers and finances did not exclude joint actions by the federal and *Länder* governments. On the contrary, the Basic Law contained from the outset numerous provisions calling for *Bund–Länder* cooperation. For example, cooperation is called for under Articles 35 and 91 of the Basic Law, which call on the federal government to assist the *Länder* governments in maintaining law and order, in averting threats to the democratic system and in dealing with natural catastrophes. In addition, there emerged out of the division of powers a distinct overlap between the two levels of *Bund* and *Länder* in the *Bundesrat* (which participates in the federal legislative process, while also representing the *Länder* governments, which are responsible for the implementation of the bulk of federal legislation). The institutional structures of West German federalism thus necessitate close and continuous cooperation between the organs of *Bund* and *Länder*. The *Länder* participate in national legislation and administration via the *Bundesrat*, while the federal government, on the other hand, possesses certain means to supervise and exert influence on the administrative practices of the *Länder* in the area of federal legislation (see Article 84 of the Basic Law).

Finally, a system of cooperation between the *Länder* has existed at minister-president and ministerial level since before the Basic Law came into effect (reflecting the fact that the *Länder* came into existence before a federation was created in the Basic Law). This system of cooperation was subsequently extended and institutionalised in various ways, as Uwe Leonardy shows in Chapter 3 of this volume.

Towards a unitary federal state

The regeneration of federalism in the Federal Republic in 1949 was no longer regarded as a means to secure the political unity of the German nation. Rather, against the background of the Third Reich, the dominant theme was the need to decentralise political power by introducing a vertical division of powers in the new West German state. For this reason, the federal principle was anchored as an inviolable principle of the Basic Law. However, the federal structures of the new state were charged, at the same time, with the task of creating uniform living conditions throughout the federal territory. The Federal Republic can thus be seen as a 'unitary federal state', a state whose institutions are federal, but whose policies, at federal and *Land* level, are oriented towards uniformity.

This prescription for uniformity does not, however, derive solely from the Basic Law, but also from broader technical and socio-economic conditions. These conditions are created, for example, by the requirements of a highly developed industrial society with its elaborate division of labour and its integrated and regionally interdependent business, transport and communications systems. It was also assumed from the outset that the population as a whole had fairly uniform expectations and demands, and would thus simply not be prepared to accept any great deviation in conditions from *Land* to *Land*.

Various means were originally conceived to ensure the maintenance of a nationwide system of common regulations which would be in the position to achieve the uniformity demanded by the unitary federal state in each policy area. Foremost among these are the uniform regulations issued by the federal government, especially in the area of legislation, but also regarding certain administrative and financial powers. It should be noted, however, that the federal government has never had *carte blanche* here. It can only act in those areas in which it is authorised to do so by the Basic Law, and, more generally, the national decision-making process is, of course, dependent on majority support in both *Bundestag* and *Bundesrat*. Secondly, functions assigned to the *Länder* in the Basic Law can be carried out on the basis of common agreement between the individual *Land* ministers responsible for particular policy areas, so that their decisions can have a uniform application throughout the country. Indeed, various forms of binding decision-making machinery and joint activities in the coordination of *Länder* policies have been developed which are based on unanimous agreement between the *Länder*. Thirdly, the federal and *Länder* governments engage in measures of cooperation and coordination in the areas of concurrent powers defined in Articles 72 and 74 of the Basic Law. This applies in particular to all questions of administrative law which usually require unanimity among the parties to the agreement. Finally, for some areas of policy, *Bund–Länder* cooperation was also constitutionally secured in the amendments to the Basic Law of 1969 and 1970, which introduced the so-called 'Joint Tasks'. These are areas in which the federal and *Länder* governments engage in joint planning, decision-making and financing, and in which, in practice, unanimous agreement between *Bund* and *Länder* is required. They are discussed more fully below.

The phase of centralisation

The period between 1949 and the beginning of the 1970s was characterised by tendencies supporting the centralisation of the West German federal system. The legislative and administrative powers of the federation were increased in particular under the terms of the granting of full sovereignty to the Federal Republic by the Western allies in 1955. Other powers were transferred from the *Länder* through constitutional amendments. An expansion of the powers of the federal government also resulted from the tendency of successive governments to interpret very broadly existing constitutional norms and to make full use of the constitutional powers assigned to the federal government.

Only a few years after the introduction of the Basic Law, it was considered necessary to adapt the constitution to changing political, economic and social conditions. In some cases the federal government assumed new responsibilities which were not originally foreseen in the Basic Law – for example, the formation of federal armed forces between 1954 and 1956 and the enactment of legislation on states of emergency in 1968. In addition, air transportation and nuclear energy were also added to the legislative and administrative responsibilities of the federation during the late 1950s and early 1960s (under Articles 87c and 87d of the Basic Law respectively). More generally, it was deemed necessary for a variety of reasons to have national regulations for a whole series of functions. As a result, there was a transfer of important legislative functions from the *Länder* to the federal government at the same time as the latter was expanding its administrative responsibilities. Financial relations between the federal and *Länder* governments were also changed in favour of the federation. By 1955–6, the originally separated taxation powers of *Bund* and *Länder* were modified through the introduction of a system of joint income and corporate taxation, and both vertical (federal grants to the *Länder*) and horizontal (transfers among the *Länder*) financial equalisation measures were expanded.

In connection with the financial reforms undertaken between 1967 and 1969, there followed a second thrust towards a redistribution of powers in favour of the federation. For considerations of national interest (primarily the need for more coherent and consistent national economic and financial policies following the recession of 1965–6), the federation was granted extra powers in budgetary and financial matters. Similarly, it was thought necessary to provide the federal government with powers appropriate to the perceived need for improved national economic management, in particular in the form of the Economic Stability and Growth Act. In addition, sales (value-added) taxes were added to the catalogue of joint taxation provisions. While the *Länder* were able at this time to expand and improve the institutions and procedures for horizontal cross-*Länder* cooperation and coordination, vertical cooperation between federal and *Länder* governments also developed beyond what was originally envisaged in the Basic Law. Cooperation and policy coordination increased in a number of policy areas (for example, in the form of administrative agreements) in the interests of a more efficient allocation of resources.

The redistribution of powers and responsibilities after 1949 thus resulted in a process of centralisation which favoured the federation at the expense of the *Länder*. Since there was never any compensation for the *Länder*, their importance as autonomous centres of political decision-making declined. This affected the organs of the *Länder* in different ways. While the legislative powers of the *Länder* parliaments were drastically reduced, the *Länder* governments experienced a rather more subtle redefinition of their functions. This is examined in the following section.

The stage of intergovernmental relations ('Politikverflechtung')

At the beginning of the 1970s, the centralisation of powers had progressed to the point that the future of the *Länder* as independent entities and, therefore, the fundamental inviolability of the federal principle in Article 79 of the Basic Law seemed to be in doubt. This necessitated a modification of the model of the 'unitary federal state' (the combination of decentralised federal institutions with uniform policies across the federation). This was effected through the introduction of 'Joint Tasks' (*'Gemeinschaftsaufgaben'*). Under these Joint Tasks, the responsible organs of *Bund* and *Länder* make use of a jointly determined authority (in planning, decision-making, finance and, to some extent, administration) oriented towards the fulfillment of certain tasks for which the *Länder* originally had exclusive responsibility under the Basic Law. These jointly planned and financed projects and measures are concerned with economic and structural issues of national importance requiring heavy infrastructural investments which would, without the involvement of the federation, place too great a financial burden on the *Länder* and the municipalities.

The anchoring of these Joint Tasks in the constitution in 1969–70 (Articles 91a and 91b of the Basic Law) resulted in a decisive change in the West German federal system. The Joint Tasks introduced a situation involving not just an intensive coordination of the relationships between

Bund and *Länder* governments, but also one involving a new factor – common implementation. Under the Joint Tasks, planning and decision-making authority, including financial responsibilities, are no longer separated between the two levels, but rather are assigned to both Federal and *Länder* governments on a common or joint basis. In other words, the clear separation of functions between *Bund* and *Länder* originally envisaged in the Basic Law gave way to intergovernmental actions under the joint responsibility of the relevant organs. This has been characterised by Fritz Scharpf as *'Politikverflechtung'*, an 'enmeshment' of the two levels of government. The dualistic conception of the federal state of 1949 thus gave way to a 'cooperative federalism'.

Since then, this *Politikverflechtung* has expanded into a regularised system of joint activity. Cooperation between federal and *Länder* governments has intensified since the beginning of the 1970s. At the same time, the coordinative network of relations between the *Länder* governments has also been strengthened. The federal and *Länder* governments thus hardly every make policy decisions alone any more. They increasingly work together on a joint basis, irrespective of which level has (in constitutional terms) the relevant legislative or administrative authority, or which level is responsible for finances. All actors are more or less involved in all decisions without any of them assuming sole responsibility.

The cooperative federal state

Results of recent developments

With the 'eternal' federalism clause in Article 79, Section 3 of the Basic Law, the founding fathers of the West German constitution declared the federal structure of the Federal Republic to be inviolable. This institutional guarantee refers, however, only to the principle of a federal system and not to any concrete arrangements for that system. Thus the nature of West German federalism, in particular the relations between *Bund* and *Länder* has, as shown above, been open to substantial change. Since 1949, there have been thirty-five amendments to the Basic Law. More than twenty of these have had a direct or indirect effect on *Bund–Länder* relations. These changes have brought about above all else an expansion of the legislative powers of the *Bund* at the expense of those of the *Länder*. This redistribution of legislative powers proved to be a 'one-way street', since the *Länder* were never compensated for their losses. The federal government was able to strengthen its position considerably, in that it used its (old and new) legislative powers extensively, and thereby greatly narrowed the legislative 'room for manoeuvre' remaining with the *Länder*. In the area of administration too, the federal government was able to increase its influence *vis-a-vis* the *Länder*. The results of these deeply rooted changes which have confronted the West German federal system since 1949 can be assessed as follows.

Firstly, the focus of legislative power, including the power of the purse, lies with the federation. However, despite the legislative influence of the federation, the *Länder* still possess extensive powers in the administration and implementation of federal legislation. Central direction combined with decentralised implementation has reduced the federal system to a kind of 'administrative federalism'. This development has been further exacerbated by the encroachment of the European Community upon the autonomy of the *Länder*, as Rudolf Hrbek shows in his contribution to this volume.

Secondly, a clear and separate distribution of functions has been replaced by joint responsibility between the two levels of government. This has resulted in an intensification of cooperation and coordination between the federation and the *Länder*. The federal state of the founding fathers with its clear demarcation between the separate levels of government in the form of a 'layer cake' has been replaced by the 'marble cake' of cooperative federalism.

Thirdly, the narrowing of the autonomy of the *Länder* which has accompanied the development of joint functions has been compensated in large part through the strengthened participation of the *Länder* in the political process at the federal level (through the *Bundesrat*) and through the network of combined *Bund–Länder* bodies and conferences (as discussed in detail by Uwe Leonardy in Chapter 3 of this volume). Co-determination in the federal area has thus, in part at least, replaced the self-determination of the *Länder*. This has had an ambivalent effect on the organs of the *Länder*. While the *Länder* governments have largely been drawn in to this process of co-determination, the *Länder* parliaments have received no compensation for the loss of their legislative autonomy.

Fourthly, the remaining administrative powers of the *Länder* are subject to the regulatory and financial powers of the federation. Policy formulation and the direction of economic and social change take place largely through the organs of the federal level. There is therefore a clear imbalance in favour of the federation in the making of public policy. Policy-making has become increasingly centralised.

Fifthly, and drawing together the above four points, the fairly well-balanced federal relationship of 1949 has been skewed by the clear loss of political power and influence by the *Länder* and the corresponding growth in federal powers. Although the institutional structures of federalism still remain much as before, the losses suffered by the *Länder* have led to a serious erosion of the substance of the West German federal system.

Consequences for the political–administrative system

The concept of cooperative federalism thus incorporates centralising tendencies and intergovernmental relations. Highly praised in the beginning as the 'ultimate wisdom' and as an 'active principle of the state' which could solve all national infrastructural problems, the cooperative federal state has since been subject to hefty criticism and is currently faced by a predominantly negative assessment both in political–administrative circles and in the academic literature. This pessimistic assessment revolves around certain negative consequences cooperative federalism has had for the political–administrative system. In particular, cooperative federalism has not been effective enough in carrying out Joint Tasks. Joint Tasks were only successful in certain limited areas, like university construction. In other areas, for example, the joint structural policies of the federal and *Länder* governments, the Joint Task framework was unable to reduce regional disparities, at best preventing only the emergence of still greater differences. It proved almost impossible to focus joint efforts in view of the rigid insistence of the *Länder* on equal treatment and their concern to protect and maintain their existing privileges. The development of the Joint Tasks is also held to have narrowed the flexibility of policy formulation in the *Länder* by imposing rigid national priorities on the regional level. But despite this reduced flexibility (or, perhaps, the increased 'disciplining') of the *Länder*, the federal government has still failed to achieve a consistent and effective national direction and coordination of structural policies.

In another sense, the attempt under the Joint Tasks to bring about structural economic reform via bureaucratic planning and coordination has attracted massive criticism due to the high administrative costs involved and the bureaucratisation of the decision-making process in both vertical (*Bund–Länder*) and horizontal (*Länder–Länder*) bureaucracies. The high level of bureaucratisation also raises problems of democratic accountability in view of the inadequate public transparency of the decision-making process and the diffusion of responsibility (and therefore accountability) in a complex, multi-faceted institutional network. Finally, the practice of cooperative federalism has tended to exclude the legislative branch, especially at the level of the *Länder*, from the decision-making process. This again raises the spectre of a 'democratic deficit' and exacerbates the problem of accountability.

Developments in the 1980s

A change of course: the Kohl Chancellorship and 'refederalisation'

The negative consequences of the system of cooperative federalism were reflected in calls for the reform of the system throughout the 1970s. However, none of these reform initiatives, whether proposed in the academic literature or within the political system itself, met with success. The 'normative power of what exists' proved stronger than all plans for change.

However, the economic problems encountered during the last years of the SPD–FDP coalition brought about the beginnings of a change of course. The attempt to fight the recession and rising unemployment with anti-cyclical budgetary and financial policies led to significant new public borrowing and expenditure programmes and to large budget deficits. This resulted, however, only in a modest and temporary economic improvement. Additional and unavoidable federal outlays for the European Community subsequently made it necessary to make massive cuts in federal spending in order to avoid a financial crisis. In an attempt to consolidate the budgetary situation, the SPD–FDP coalition cut federal investment expenditure in particular. This affected above all federal grants for the Joint Tasks and mixed *Bund–Länder* financing programmes. Subsequently, federal funds for financing Joint Tasks were cut, on average, by about 20 per cent. At the same time, the federal government insisted on maintaining the Joint Tasks system as it stood, in order not to lose the possibility of maintaining a potential for coordinated national economic management and for exerting influence over the setting of priorities in the *Länder*. This ambivalent position – a clear case of the federal government 'having its cake and eating it' – inevitably led to tensions between the federal government and the *Länder*, which was expressed in particular in an escalating conflict between the SPD–FDP federal government and the opposition CDU/CSU majority in the *Bundesrat*.

The result was a progressive erosion of both the spirit and the system of cooperative federalism. Federal government and *Länder* subsequently agreed in principle that the system of intergovernmental relations should be curtailed, the federal government in particular stressing the need for a clearer separation of functions between the two levels of government. This it underlined by withdrawing unilaterally from the Joint Tasks of housing provision and financial aid for students. Although the negotiations between the federal government and the *Länder* ultimately collapsed over the financial implications of a separation of functions (i.e. the redistribution of funds after the reduction of mixed financing), a clear 'wind of change' had made itself felt in *Bund–Länder* relations.

This was confirmed in the autumn of 1982 with the formation of a new federal government coalition, uniting the CDU/CSU with the FDP, under Chancellor Helmut Kohl. In his Government Declaration, Kohl stressed the Christian Democratic principle of subsidiarity, and stated his intention of giving this principle practical effect by enabling the *Länder* to assume responsibility for those tasks which they could fulfil more effectively than the federal government. Since the constitutionally guaranteed autonomy of the *Länder* was, it was suggested, designed to keep a distant central government at bay, the powers of the federal government were no longer to be interpreted extensively at the cost of the *Länder*. This was underlined in the coalition agreement between the CDU/CSU and FDP, where the new government promised to limit mixed financing programmes in order to promote a clear separation of tasks between the federal and the *Länder* governments.

The Kohl government thus introduced, from the first day onwards, a new tone into *Bund–Länder* relations. After thirteen years of discord, the same party coalition possess majorities in both *Bundestag* and *Bundesrat*. Kohl advocated a close, and certainly more harmonious cooperation between his government and the *Länder*. The positive reaction in the *Bundesrat* to these overtures underscored the reduced tension in the relations between *Bund* and *Länder*. The 'new era' was further underlined by the fact that several members of the Kohl government had emerged from leadership positions in the *Länder* and were both familiar with and sympathetic to the work of the *Bundesrat*.

The new approach of Kohl had direct and practical consequences in several arenas. The increased prominence given to the concerns of the *Länder* was reflected in the instalment of a State Secretary with broad responsibilities for federal issues within the Federal Chancellor's Office. Moreover, the federal government made special efforts in the area of financing to accommodate the *Länder*. This could be seen in the redistribution of revenues from sales taxes, whereby the federal government agreed to increase the share of the *Länder* by 2 per cent. Since, at the same time, supplementary federal grants to the poorer *Länder* were also retained, the *Länder* found themselves in a much better financial position than would have prevailed if the previous SPD/FDP federal government had remained in office. In addition, the federal investment funds and subsidies for the *Länder* which had been cut by the SPD/FDP coalition were reinstated and even increased over past levels. For the 1983 budget, federal funds for joint tasks were thus increased to some DM 500 million more than the previous budget proposals of the Schmidt government.

In order to promote economic growth, the federal government also started up a DM 2.5 billion programme of public housing construction for 1983 and 1984, which included a subsidy of some DM 100 million for student housing (an area of *Länder* responsibility). The federal government also announced a more cautious approach in the legislative arena which would take care to meet the concerns of the *Länder*. Bills were to take the legitimate interests of the *Länder* into consideration from an early stage, and it was hoped that this early consultation would promote agreement with the *Länder* and the *Bundesrat* and thus obviate the need to convene the *Bundestag–Bundesrat* Mediation Committee.

In the case of Joint Tasks and mixed financing, the heads of the federal and *Länder* governments were able relatively quickly to come to an agreement which at least partially restored *Länder* autonomy. The federal government agreed both to restrict its own financial interventions to those areas explicitly specified in the Joint Task legislation and to restore previous levels of funds granted to the *Länder*. These measures clearly demonstrated the strength of the Minister-Presidents of the *Länder* ruled by the CDU/CSU who had increasingly established themselves as a centre of political leadership during the years of CDU/CSU opposition in the *Bundestag*.

The results of refederalisation: disentanglement and decentralisation

This change, of course, while introducing a new trend in the federal system, did not, however, amount to a complete break with the past. Any redistribution of legislative powers in favour of the *Länder* or a more thoroughgoing reform, or even abolition of the Joint Tasks system would have required amendments to the Basic Law. Since the necessary *Bundestag* majority for constitutional amendments did and still does not exist, such fundamental changes in the relations between *Bund* and *Länder* governments are not to be expected (unless they can be agreed upon in the constitutional discussions which will accompany and follow the accession of the GDR to the Federal Republic during the early 1990s). However, the more strongly *Länder*-oriented policies of the Kohl government have had important consequences, which can be summarised under the headings of deregulation, or disentanglement, and decentralisation.

Probably the most important effect of Kohl's initiatives was the disentanglement of the joint responsibilities associated with mixed financing programmes. Following protracted negotiations between the federal and *Länder* governments over policies towards students in higher education, the construction of student residences was removed from the system of mixed financing and became the sole financial responsibility of the *Länder* (although some federal funding was retained in the area of university students' financial support). The most important example of disentanglement, however, concerned hospital construction. Within the framework of reorganising hospitals policy, the *Länder* alone have been responsible for the planning and financing of hospital construction since January 1985. The federal government has surrendered its power in this area and ceased its financial participation.

Another example of disentanglement is to be found in the federal government's withdrawal from the educational planning process under Article 91b of the Basic Law. Towards the end of the Schmidt era in 1982, the federal government and the *Bund–Länder* Education Commission were no longer able to agree on a continuation of the General Education Plan of 1973. Partisan differences between Education and Finance Ministers in different *Länder* regarding educational priorities prevented any consensus from emerging. As a consequence, the subsequent CDU/CSU–FDP government and the CDU/CSU-governed *Länder* decided to withdraw from general education planning, and the *Bund–Länder* Education Commission was dissolved. Educational planning was thus restored to the autonomous authority of the individual *Länder*, as was the coordination of education policy to the Conference of *Länder* Ministers of Education. As an exception, the promotion of scientific research activities was maintained as an area of joint planning and finance, although cuts were made both in staffing levels and in projects supported.

A final field under consideration for disentanglement is federal support for urban renewal and public housing. Under the new Federal Construction Code, effective as of 1 January 1988, the *Länder* have been given the authority to regulate certain areas on their own. Although federal investment grants of some DM 660 million are to be continued, they are only to be used in the area of the housing policy to promote private housebuilding. In the area of public rented housing, however, the federal government is to withdraw in favour of the independent authority of the *Länder*.

As noted above, a formal decentralisation of legislative powers in favour of the *Länder* cannot be introduced without constitutional amendment. However, a *de facto* decentralisation can occur through the legislative 'self-restraint' of the federal government. In this way, legislative responsibility for educational assistance programmes for schoolchildren has been left over by the Kohl government to the *Länder*, which have now begun to pass their own statutes in this area. It could, nonetheless, quite correctly be said that the practice by the federal government of creating substantially greater legislative flexibility for the *Länder* by restricting its own claim on legislative powers is one-sided and reversible at any time. However, federal restraint has been further encouraged by a change in the operating procedures of the federal ministries. Proposals for federal laws are now examined both in the Chancellor's Office and in the ministries themselves to see whether federal legislation is really necessary in each individual case. The federal civil service in Bonn is therefore forced to provide comprehensive justification for each separate federal legislative proposal. As a result, there is an in-built check on the previous tendency of federal governments to interpret rather over-zealously the ambit of federal legislative responsibilities under Article 72 of the Basic Law (concerning legislative powers held concurrently with the *Länder*).

Limits to the reform strategy

As accurate prognosis as to whether and to what extent the Kohl government's strategy of reforming cooperative federalism arrangements will be continued is difficult to make. However, it does appear that certain limits to this reform strategy can already be identified.

Most generally, it appears that the pro-*Länder* atmosphere which characterised the early phase of the Kohl government has begun to dissipate in day-to-day practice. New disputes over the division of authority and conflicts regarding financial interests have burdened the initially more harmonious relationship between *Bund* and *Länder*. It has become clear that coordination within the Chancellor's Office has not always been smooth. Moreover, relations between the federal government and the *Länder* governed by the SPD have been characterised by a deep-seated conflict arising from basic political differences and from the practice of pursuing essentially federal electoral ends at regional level in the regular *Land* elections which are held between *Bundestag* elections. Tensions and controversies in the relations between the federal government and the *Länder* governed by the Christian Democrats have also undermined the far-reaching consensus which prevailed in the early Kohl era.

More important in producing a change in the Kohl government's initial orientation towards the *Länder* are, however, certain structural factors which have begun to sour the relationship between *Bund* and *Länder*. In developing coherent national economic and structural policies, in particular in view of continued problems concerning agriculture and regional economic disparities, the federal government is dependent on the actions of the *Länder* and municipalities, which are responsible for the administration of 70 per cent of all public capital investment in the country. In order to promote economic growth, therefore, the federal government has had to reactivate the use of federal assistance for the

Länder in certain policy areas. For these reasons, the federal government has provided the *Länder* with DM 2.5 billion in grants for housing construction and student residences and in 1985 increased its investment grants for urban development by DM 1 billion for 1986–7. It has also become evident that research and technological development will require more state support in view of rapid technological change in certain fields. This has resulted in the devising of a new joint *Bund–Länder* programme for the promotion of high-level research amounting to more than DM 150 million. This renewed 'invasion' of the *Bund* into what had initially been seen by the Kohl government as concerns of the *Länder* has been accompanied by increased intervention by the federal government in the area of the mass media. Here, one of the last areas of *Länder* authority as originally envisaged in the Basic Law which has largely remained free from federal incursions, the federal government has attempted, for technical reasons, to use its authority to regulate telecommunications as a means of directing the reorganisation of radio and television as well as the development of new media forms. As a result, media policy is already being mooted in Bonn as a new Joint Task, whereby the federal government is attempting to win over the *Länder* and municipalities as partners in a new cooperative approach.

It is thus clear that the *Bund* is once more encroaching on the autonomy of the *Länder* in the areas of structural and mass media policy. *Länder* autonomy has also been reduced in other areas for wholly different reasons. These relate to the application by the governing coalition of the philosophy of 'more market and less state' in certain policy areas (a philosophy not, however, consistently applied, as can be seen from the areas examined above!). This philosophy suggests that, in general, state functions are to be transferred to the private sector and that private investment is to be given precedence over public investment. It has been applied particularly in revisions to the University Framework law and in reorganising the hospital system (areas under partial *Länder* authority), where the federal government has consistently attempted to transfer regulatory authority to the private sector or to self-governing units of administration. In this process, the *Länder* still emerge as losers, as not only federal but also *Länder* responsibilities are transferred to other bodies.

Further *Bund–Länder* problems have been encountered in the area of financing. In some cases, the federal government has retreated from performing certain functions jointly with the *Länder* without showing any willingness to reach a compensatory financial adjustment with the *Länder*. If the *Länder* are then faced with new financial burdens, the financial imbalance between the two state levels will be exacerbated even more to the detriment of the *Länder*. These various aspects of the recent situation together point out the limited potential of reform strategies which have as their goal a modification of the division of powers between *Bund* and *Länder*. It seems, therefore, that any future changes in *Bund–Länder* relations will be, at best, of only a limited, incremental nature.

The new trend: federally oriented policies

The limits to the Kohl government's federal reform strategy thus became apparent rather more quickly than one might have imagined. As a result, the federal government has not been able to maintain the same friendly relations with the *Länder* which it enjoyed at the outset. This has especially been so since the start of the new legislative period in 1987, since when there has been a return to a focus on policies oriented towards the needs of the federal government. Major federal problems, like tax reforms, social security and the creation of the EC Single Market, have taken political precedence. With such pressing concerns, the *Länder* are now seen by the federal government, and in particular the FDP, as obstacles which, if necessary, are to be ignored.

There has also been a perceptible increase within the *Länder* themselves in the potential for conflict with the federal government. Even those *Länder* governed by the same parties represented in the federal government tend to express their special regional interests forcefully, even intransigently, without paying particular attention to the priorities of the Bonn coalition. This is in part the result of the behaviour of *Länder* politicians (W. Steffani speaks, for example, of the 'republic of *Land* princes'), but even more so it reflects the genuine interests of the individual *Länder*. In the areas of finances and legislative power, the *Länder* feel themselves, as shown above, to be constrained by, or under pressure from Bonn. Pressure creates counter-pressure, which then leads to irritation within the federal government, which perceives itself to be under the threat of 'extortion' by the *Länder*. The CDU-led *Länder* governments of Baden-Württemberg and Hesse have exacerbated these tensions by contesting the recent provision of federal grants to the nine economically weaker *Länder* (including West Berlin) before the Federal Constitutional Court. It is, however, characteristic of this kind of conflict that differences are discussed in informal circles associated with the coalition parties before they emerge on institutional agendas. In particular, the federal coalition has attempted to keep conflict out of the *Bundesrat*, and above all away from the *Bundestag–Bundesrat* Mediation Committee, in order to minimise the potential influence of the SPD-governed *Länder* and the SPD and Green opposition factions in the *Bundestag*.

Financial and structural problems

The current relationship between the federal and *Länder* governments is dominated by financial problems. In spite of favourable economic conditions, above-average tax revenues and sizable profits from the activities of the *Bundesbank*, federal borrowing has been disproportionately high. Increased payments to the European Community, outlays for unemployment support and a broadly based tax reform have led to growing budget deficits. Furthermore, the planned restructuring of the social security system (health insurance and old age pensions) will require enormous additional expenditure. These financial restrictions faced by the federal government preclude any substantial concessions to the *Länder*. Indeed, federal grants and assistance programmes for the *Länder* are now being cut once more as a consequence of the financial difficulties of the federal government. This applies, for example, both to urban renewal programmes and to public housing. In addition, supplementary grants for capital investment are being phased out. Federal funding has been increased for supplementary grants within the scheme of fiscal equalisation, for the Joint Task programme of regional economic development and for the grants mentioned above for nine of the eleven *Länder*, but these all apply only for a limited period of time and compensate very inadequately for the cut in *Länder* funds available for capital investment which will result from the current tax reform programme (which concentrate on raising indirect taxation at the expense of direct taxation and benefit the federal government disproportionately).

The *Länder* too are confronted by a mountain of economic problems. Even before now, their financial resources were inadequate, and this inadequacy has grown as more responsibilities have to be taken on as federal assistance is reduced. As noted above, the *Länder* will also lose out from the current tax reform programme. With their revenue base in direct taxation falling, the *Länder* are becoming increasingly dependent on whatever federal subsidies are still being granted. It is not surprising, then, that the *Länder* feel more and more like pawns of the federal government. These trends could be reversed by an increase in the share of indirect (sales) tax receipts distributed to the *Länder*, but this is unlikely in face of the many other demands placed on such revenues. In the meantime, the contrast between the 'rich' and 'poor' *Länder*, the so-called 'North–South gap', has sharpened. Even within the individual *Länder* there are serious disparities between industrialised and rural areas. The greater social welfare costs faced by the economically weaker *Länder* have acted as an additional drag. Even though federal grants cannot be expected to alleviate all of these problems, it will surely be necessary to develop some new policies to promote investment and combat regional inequalities.

Renewed intergovernmentalisation

There have recently been very clear signs of reversion on the part of the federal government to an increased emphasis on nationally oriented policies under the framework of the Joint Tasks. The reform of cooperative federalism in the direction of a greater separation of functions, in particular through reductions in mixed financing, has been stopped or reversed due to shortages of public housing in metropolitan areas, the problems of coping with excessive numbers of students in the universities and the structural problems faced by older, declining industrial regions. In order to solve these problems, the federal government is attempting to revive the joint financing of these activities. Particularly prominent examples are the special programme of public housing for newly arrived migrants from the East, new funds for the support of universities and the new grants for the nine economically weaker *Länder*. Recently disentangled programmes, such as public housing and urban development, are being transformed into new versions of mixed financing. These activities of the federal government within the framework of joint financing schemes are once again increasing the influence of the federal government in areas of *Länder* responsibility

Centralising tendencies

In addition to the above, there are increasing tendencies to strengthen the position of the federal government *vis-à-vis* the *Länder* through the imposition of uniform federal regulations. An example of this is the demand by the Federal Minister for Education for new framework powers in educational matters as a response to European Community regulations, even though this is a key area of *Länder* autonomy. Similarly, the Minister of Justice has asserted federal authority in respect of public liability law and gene technology. Taken together, these steps would seem to indicate that federal government has gone on the offensive in seeking new powers.

Three other factors should be taken into account when considering the current state of German federalism. The first concerns the catalogue of basic rights which are guaranteed in the Basic Law. These apply equally to all citizens in all *Länder* of the Federal Republic. This has the effect of promoting uniformity at the expense of the diversity associated with a federal system by requiring the *Länder* to coordinate their legal

policies in accordance with national standards. This requirement under-
lies the current controversy concerning the obligations of the *Länder* to
harmonise their policies regarding the regulation of the mass media.

Secondly, major projects involving the employment of modern technology (for example, nuclear power plants and nuclear waste disposal),
environmental protection measures and other activities of various kinds
which transcend *Länder* boundaries (for example, radio and TV transmission) have a direct effect on the federal system by promoting a
diversion of powers from the *Länder* to the federal government in the
interests of attaining common national standards and improving
national coordination. A recent example would be the federal law on
radioactive pollution, which has introduced uniform federal regulations
in response to the confusion and public protests which resulted from the
different and often conflicting reactions of the various *Länder* to the
nuclear accident at Chernobyl.

Finally, an even greater challenge for the *Länder* is represented by the
continuing progress towards European integration through the Single
European Act and the Single Market of 1992. For the Federal Republic,
the European Community has become a second arena, additional to the
existing arena of *Bund–Länder* relations, requiring cooperation and coordination on the part of the federal government and its administrative
organs, creating what Fritz Scharpf has termed 'double intergovernmental relations'. It is clear that the political costs paid in the course of closer
European integration will be paid primarily by the *Länder*. The *Länder*
have already lost, or are likely to lose powers due to EC regulations in
the areas of regional economic development, education and the mass
media. The procedures for *Bundesrat* participation in the consultation
and decision-making processes of the EC cannot substitute for real and
potential losses of *Länder* autonomy.

The current situation, therefore, is not a promising one for supporters of *Länder* autonomy. Throughout its existence, the Federal
Republic has undergone a progressive, if uneven, process of centralisation, which has proved impervious even to the initial attempts of the
Kohl government to 'refederalise' the system. With this in mind, it would
not, perhaps, be an exaggeration to suggest that behind the federal
façade, a largely unitary and centralised state form has been established
in the Federal Republic.

Note

1. An earlier version of this chapter, entitled 'Forty years of German federa-
    lism: past trends and new developments' appeared in *Publius. The Journal of
    Federalism*, **19** (1989), 185–202.

Into the 1990s: Federalism and German unification

8

Uwe Leonardy

The most hotly debated topic in German politics and constitutional development at present is without doubt the question of German unification. The chain of events which was sparked off by the dismantling of the Hungarian iron curtain in September 1989, and which led to the peaceful revolution in the GDR and the opening of the frontier between the two Germanies on 9 November 1989, has drastically changed the context of German politics as we enter the 1990s.[1] As a result, a whole series of proposals has been put forward since November 1989 in an attempt to plot out the future political, constitutional and economic development of a united Germany.

This is not the appropriate place to evaluate these often controversial schemes and concepts for German unification. One thing can, however, be said of the whole unification debate: the fact that the fundamental pattern of German unity will be a federal one. Regardless of how and when unity is achieved, one of the first constitutional measures to be taken by the German Democratic Republic following the elections of 18 March 1990 will inevitably be the re-establishment of the *Länder* within her territory. The basis of this process may well be the federal structure which existed in the GDR until 1952, when the *Länder* of Mecklenburg, Brandenburg, Saxe-Anhalt, Thuringia and Saxony were abolished by the communist regime in favour of centralised administrative districts. Prior to their abolition, the East German *Länder* were represented, by members of the *Land* legislatures, in a *Länderkammer*, which served in a capacity similar to that of the *Bundesrat*.[2]

The federal relevance of the unification process centres on two fields. The first of these – and the factor of the most immediate current impact – is the participation of the West German *Länder* in the decision-making process leading to a unified and federal Germany. The second, following from this, concerns the changes German federalism will have to undergo after unity has been achieved in order to maintain both the effectiveness and acceptability of its working structures. The opportunities and challenges of the process of 'growing together that which belongs together' (Willy Brandt) within a federal system will largely revolve around these two fields.

Participation of the West German *Länder* in the unification process

The relations between the two German states both developed within a multi-faceted framework of rapidly growing bilateral, East–West German cooperation and negotiation and also have considerable implications on the European Community level. The *Länder* of the Federal Republic are naturally seeking to maintain and instrumentalise further their share of decision-making in both of these arenas. As was shown in Chapter 3, the *Länder* have already taken steps to ensure that both their influence in EC affairs and their implications for German federalism are felt. Any future consideration by the EC of problems concerning the GDR will serve to underline this.

In a *Bundesrat* debate on 21 December 1989[3] the West German *Länder* also gave clear expression to their claim for consultation and participation in any East–West German deliberations with regard to the emergence of a constitutional structure comprising the two Germanies and their component federal parts. Irrespective of political affiliation, speakers urged the Federal Government to secure for the *Länder* both an adequate supply of information as well as effective means of participation not only in negotiations with the GDR but also in all joint institutional bodies set up to facilitate the process of cooperation and joint decision-making leading to German unity.

In justifying their claim, the *Länder* were in the fortunate position of being able to refer to a formal 'Agreement between the Federal and *Länder* Governments on the Participation of the *Länder* Concerning Agreements between the Federal Republic of Germany and the German Democratic Republic', which had already been signed by the Conference of the Federal Chancellor with the Heads of Government of the *Länder* on 17 December 1987. The *Länder* were formally assured of the Federal Government's continued willingness to cooperate closely on GDR matters on the basis of this Agreement. This was underlined by the Chancellor in his Conference with the Heads of the *Länder* Governments, which took place immediately after the aforementioned *Bundesrat* debate of 21 December 1989. Bearing in mind that certain problems, especially that of continued migration from the GDR to the Federal Republic, were felt most concretely at *Land* and local government level, there could, in fact, be no doubt about the increasing necessity of such cooperation. This point was strongly emphasised by the *Länder* in a Conference of the Chief of the Chancellor's Office with his counterparts in the *Länder* on 30 January 1990, because the *Länder* felt that their participation, despite all assurances, had not been sufficiently provided for by the Federal Government up to that date. As a result, the Conference agreed that in future it would meet monthly to coordinate matters on this and all related topics. This apparently extensive opportunity for *Länder* participation was, however, qualified by the reference by the Chief of the Chancellor's Office to the Agreement of December 1987, and his statement that the Federal Government would examine the need, on the basis of this Agreement, for the consultation of the *Länder* prior to each individual agreement with the GDR. The *Länder* felt that this might marginalise their participation, in that the entire process of 'growing together' would substantially change the basis on which the 1987 Agreement had been shaped and might thus undermine the right to participation and consultation enshrined for them in the Agreement.

After some public controversy, the *Länder* succeeded in asserting their point of view in a revised and widened Agreement between the Chancellor and the Heads of the *Länder* Governments, which was formulated in their Conference of 15th February 1990. The Agreement contained the following major points.

Firstly, the *Länder* are to participate in the preparation of future constitutional and administrative structures on terms of equal status with the Federation. They thus have the right of equal representation on all the various bodies and commissions – extant or yet to be created – dealing with such matters in the Federal Republic.

Secondly, during the process of negotiations with the GDR, the Federal Government is to inform the *Länder* fully and continuously about all relevant issues. To underline this, the Heads of the *Länder* Cabinet Offices have become a 'Permanent Body' which is to serve as a partner of the Federation in all matters concerning Germany unity.

Thirdly, the Federal Government is to give the *Länder* the opportunity to present their collective view, after consultation with each other, before final decisions are taken in any relevant matters.

Fourthly, negotiations with the GDR are to be conducted by the Federal Government on the basis of the 1987 Agreement, with the regular participation of representatives of the *Länder*.

Fifthly, the *Länder* are to participate both in such negotiations and in the various joint bodies and commissions which will be established together with the GDR. They are to be represented by the Chairman of the Conference of Minister-Presidents and by one speaker for that group of *Länder* to which the Chairman does not belong in terms of party-political affiliation. Both of these two representatives can delegate their functions. If the interests of specific *Länder* are involved, such *Länder* are to have additional representation.

Sixthly, negotiations are to be chaired by the *Länder* if their subject matter lies within the sphere of exclusive *Länder* competence. In such cases, Federation and *Länder* are to be represented on the respective bodies or delegations on an equal basis.

Seventhly, the Federal Government has agreed to 'take note' of the intention of the Heads of the *Länder* Governments to call a Conference of Minister-Presidents of all German *Länder* as soon as federal structures are restored in the GDR.

Whether these various arrangements for *Länder* participation actually come to fruition within the somewhat hectic atmosphere surrounding the unification process remains to be seen. Nevertheless, since this agreement was formulated, the participation of the *Länder* has been at least partly realised in the following areas.

The *Länder* have been included in Federal Government Working Groups dealing with the preparations for future constitutional and administrative structures and on legal matters which fall under the responsibility of a newly established Federal Cabinet Committee for German Unity.

The *Länder* have also been accorded partial representation on joint bodies and commissions established together with the GDR in the fields of economic relations, transport, post and telecommunications, environmental affairs, safety of nuclear energy production, legal affairs, building matters and cultural affairs (where they have claimed the chair). They have, however, been excluded from participation in deliberations and negotiations concerning the establishment of currency union with the GDR. In all the policy fields in which they are represented they have taken the necessary steps to secure a regular exchange of information between their representatives and the respective conferences of the *Länder* ministers who have equivalent policy responsibilities.

In a quid pro quo for their participation in the deliberations and negotiations of the Federal Government, the *Länder* have agreed to report regularly on their own independent, direct regional contacts and activities in the GDR in the monthly Conference of the Heads of the Chancellor's and the *Länder* Cabinet Offices. These contacts and activities include partnerships with the districts in the territories of the old *Länder* in the East, such as Schleswig-Holstein has established with the districts of what was formerly Mecklenburg, Lower Saxony with those of former Saxe-Anhalt, Hesse with those of former Thuringia, Baden-Württemberg and Bavaria with those of former Saxony, West Berlin with those of former Brandenburg and, of course, with East Berlin. Regional committees and liaison officers have been established under the terms of these partnerships, and *Länder* funds have been made available to carry out urgent measures in fields such as health, environment, transport, housing, economic aid and administrative advice. In view of these activities, direct intervention, at regional level, by the Federal Government in cooperation with the government of the GDR has not, consequently, been encouraged by the *Länder*.

In general terms, the *Bundesrat* has warmly welcomed the re-emergence of a federal structure in the GDR and has put forward strong claims for its participation in this process. However, in a debate of 16 February 1990,[4] it rejected an institutional initiative launched by North-Rhine-Westphalia, which aimed to set up a Joint Committee of *Bundestag* and *Bundesrat* with the remit of preparing, in cooperation with the Federal Government,[5] all constitutional decisions connected with the re-establishment of German unity. An equivalent initiative was proposed simultaneously by the SPD faction in the *Bundestag* concerning the creation of a joint body along the lines of the Committee of Mediation, with eleven members from each of the two houses.[6] The Federal Government, together with the CDU/CSU–FDP coalition in the *Bundestag* and 'their' *Länder* in the *Bundesrat* rejected this idea. They did so on the basis that there were no constitutional grounds for any such joint body in the Basic Law, and that the institutional structures of both houses would offer sufficient leeway and opportunity for *Bundestag* and *Bundesrat* to participate in the unification process.

There is thus no political consensus on any such far-reaching institutional innovations on the federal level. However, elsewhere, the Conference of the Presidents of the *Land* Legislatures was able to agree on a Resolution on 22 February 1990 in Berlin which demanded that two representatives of this Conference should take part in the work of the joint bodies established by the Agreement of the Chancellor and the Heads of the *Länder* Government of 15 February 1990 concerning future constitutional structures. This Resolution also demanded that 'a joint parliamentary body consisting of representatives of the *Bundestag*, of the newly elected *Volkskammer* and of all German *Land* legislatures' be set up 'to coordinate the necessary political and practical steps [in the process of unification] and to participate in the building up of federal structures'. The Presidents of the *Land* Legislatures justified their demands by stressing that the legislatures represented by them 'must make use of their powers and capabilities in order to give "neighbourly" help, at *Land* level, in the building up of a representative parliamentary system in the GDR'.

While little of substance is likely to follow from these proposals, the parliamentary parties in the *Bundestag* have begun to undertake, on their own independent initiative, practical measures to consolidate the emergence of East German democracy. For example, the SPD has set up in

Berlin a branch of its *Bund–Länder* Coordination Office (attached to the parliamentary party in Bonn), with the task of giving organisational aid and practical advice to its new sister party in the *Volkskammer*, and, in more general terms, to the GDR–SPD throughout the East German territory in all matters concerned with the emergence of federal structures.

This multitude of practical steps and proposals for participation in the process of achieving German unity, in particular with regard to its federal aspects, should not, however, conceal the fact that this process will be carried out above all on the level of intragovernmental and intergovernmental relations. If unification takes place under the terms of Article 23 of the Basic Law – as seems highly likely[7] – the terms of an accession of the GDR to the Federal Republic[8] will be the subject of negotiations between the Federal Government and the new Council of Ministers in the GDR. While the new East German Parliaments will have a considerable say in the process of accession – both in defining its conditions and expectations concerning accession and in voting on the formal act of accession itself – the roles of the *Bundesrat* and *Bundestag* will be much more limited. These will be restricted essentially to the passing of statutory measures designed to facilitate the accession and of the vast range of transitional regulations which will undoubtedly be necessary.

However, these steps are very likely to require some amendments to the Basic Law and will therefore need the support of two-thirds majorities in both *Bundestag* and *Bundesrat*. This means that some form of political consensus will have to be achieved both between the CDU/CSU–FDP coalition and the SPD opposition in the *Bundestag*, and also between the entire *Länder* community in the *Bundesrat* and the Federal Government. It is clear, therefore, that although final decisions will ultimately be taken by the Federal Government, the views of the *Bundestag* and *Länder* will have to be taken into account from an early stage.

German federalism after unification

The changes which German federalism will have to undergo after the achievement of unity will revolve primarily around the two 'problem areas' which were initially discussed in Chapter 3: the territorial organisation of the federal system and the ability of that system to achieve and maintain equal living standards within and across its component parts.

At present, deliberations on the re-establishment of a federal structure in the GDR are still essentially directed towards the refoundation of the five *Länder* which existed before 1952: Mecklenburg, Brandenburg,

Thuringia, Saxony and Saxe-Anhalt. However, there has been growing public discussion regarding the creation of larger territorial units in at least two regions.[9] Proposals have been aired which would amalgamate the urban area of Berlin with the former *Land* of Brandenburg, either in conjunction with, or following a reunification of East and West Berlin.[10] Similarly, in North Germany, it has been proposed that a new East–West German *Land* consisting of old Mecklenburg, Schleswig-Holstein and Hamburg should be formed.[11] On the other hand, and moving in the opposite direction of small territorial units, there have also been occasional calls for the demarcation of the cities of Leipzig and Rostock from their former *Länder* of Saxony and Mecklenburg in order to create new city-states analagous to Hamburg and Bremen.[12]

If the old (pre-1952) *Länder* of the GDR were simply refounded with no territorial changes except the creation of a new *Land* comprising unified Berlin, the number of federal units in the new Germany would total sixteen. This would seem too high to secure an effectively functioning federal system within the relatively small territory which even a united Germany[13] would represent (certainly compared to other successful federal systems like the United States, Canada, Brazil or Australia).[14] This applies all the more so since the population density and, consequently, the degree of regional interdependence, is on average much higher in Germany than in the other federal states mentioned above.[15]

Even if we leave aside such cross-country comparisons, there are other pressing reasons, stemming from the peculiarities of the German situation, which would seem to support the demand for territorial reform both in the GDR and in the existing territorial demarcation within the Federal Republic. The process of unification provides an ideal opportunity for such reforms to be carried out.

Firstly, the dual structure of the Whole State (*Gesamtstaat*) and the Federal State (*Bundesstaat*) would scarcely be able to fulfil its functions either in an efficient or in a democratically transparent manner if it were to consist of sixteen *Länder* alongside the enlarged federation. As was shown in Chapter 3, the existing system in the Federal Republic alone is already facing very strong criticisms because of its complexity and impenetrability to the public eye.

Secondly, if the *Länder* as a whole, and in particular those to be (re)established in the GDR, wish to maintain and even enlarge their share of decision-making in European Community matters at both the federal and EC levels, they will have to secure not only their collective ability, but also their individual administrative capacity to do so. Present doubts about the ability of the West German *Länder* to meet this challenge[16] would be multiplied if too many relatively weak units were added to the system.

Thirdly, much of the same would apply with regard to the internal ability of the federal system to achieve and maintain intraregional and interregional equilibrium within and between its component parts. The difficulties already experienced in the Federal Republic in providing for uniform living standards would be massively exacerbated if the old *Länder* of the GDR were simply to be refounded as they existed before. The largest potential East German *Land*, Saxony, with 4.8 million inhabitants would be only the sixth largest *Land* in a united Germany.[17] The remainder would be significantly smaller in terms of population (united Berlin with 3.3 million inhabitants, Saxe-Anhalt with 3.0, Brandenburg with 2.7, Thuringia with 2.5 and Mecklenburg with 2.1). Moreover, there are already five *Länder* in the Federal Republic with a correspondingly small size (Rhineland-Palatinate with 3.7 million inhabitants, Schleswig-Holstein with 2.6, Hamburg with 1.6, Saarland with 1.1, and Bremen with only 0.7 million).

The need for territorial reform[18] becomes even more imperative if one considers the fact that some of the current West German (and future East German) *Länder* boundaries represent severe impediments to intraregional cooperation by cutting across densely populated and economically interlinked areas in no less than five parts of the (future) federation: in the urban regions of Hamburg, Bremen and (united) Berlin as well as in the Rhine-Main and Rhine-Neckar regions.

The immediate consequence of these considerable problems in the present and future territorial demarcation of German federalism would seem to be the need to reform the legislative procedure for the redrafting of *Länder* boundaries under Article 29 of the Basic Law, as part of the package of constitutional amendments which will precede or accompany the process of the GDR's accession to the Federal Republic under Article 23. As was indicated in Chapter 3, the powers under Article 29 concerning territorial reform were diluted in 1976. Moreover, the procedure by which territorial reform can be achieved was also vastly complicated at this time.[19] Were this to be left unchanged now, then both the enhanced need and the unique opportunity for territorial reform in both parts of Germany could hardly be carried through.

The problem of territorial demarcation and reform is closely interlinked with the second 'problem area' isolated above: the ability of the system as a whole to achieve and maintain equal standards of living within and between its constituent parts. In the future, the ability to attain such economic equilibrium will be even more strongly dependent than hitherto on the arrangements for financial redistribution both between *Bund* and *Länder* and between the *Länder* themselves.

It hardly needs to be stressed that economic conditions are incomparably worse and economic needs incomparably greater in the GDR than they are in the Federal Republic. It is almost impossible at present to produce any reliable quantification of the resources needed to balance these vast differences in standards of living and economic potential. It is certain though that the 'financial constitution' of federal financial arrangements will, for a long time, have to offer massive subsidies to the new East German *Länder* (although this may be mitigated to some extent by aid from the European Community, in particular from its Regional Fund). While this problem has long been recognised, it nevertheless incorporates considerable dangers for the development of the federal system in the next few years. In short, the longer the time-span of the need for massive financial redistribution, the more the *Bund* will have the opportunity to employ its financial 'golden lead' and thereby to increase its intervention in areas which are, constitutionally at least, responsibilities of the *Länder*. Moreover, the larger the number of 'needy' *Länder*, the stronger will be the impact of the 'golden lead' on the federal system as a whole. This could introduce a prolonged period of centralisation in German federalism such as happened in the years following the foundation of the Federal Republic through to the financial reforms of 1966–9. To prevent such a development, the number of the newly emerging *Länder* in East Germany will have to be kept as small as possible, and the sum total of East and West German *Länder* combined will have to be reduced.

In addition, constitutional safeguards against abuses of the 'golden lead' will have to be included among the revisions to the Basic Law which will be necessary during the process of unification. These safeguards could include constitutional definitions of the financial needs of the poorer *Länder* in order to save them from having to negotiate away autonomy in return for financial 'rewards'. They could also include the abolition, or at least modification of the present rule that the federation can pass legislation which imposes financial burdens upon the *Länder* with the consent of only a simple majority in the *Bundesrat*.[20] Some modification of the majority needed in the *Bundesrat* for measures like this could act as additional protection not only for the poorer *Länder*, but also of the *Länder* community as a whole against the encroachment of the *Bund*.

In the forthcoming months and years, an intense exchange of views and opinions on these two fields of federal development will unfold between East and West Germany. The same applies to the existing federal network of working relations in the West and the potential adaptations which will have to be made to accommodate the East. In particular, there will be a growing demand from the emerging *Länder* in East Germany for access to the practical experience accumulated in the structures of *Bund–Länder* and *Länder–Länder* relations in West Germany.

The reinstitution of federalism on the territory of the GDR is going to absorb and invigorate political and administrative energies both there and in West Germany for years to come. All the component parts of the federal structure in West Germany will be prepared to advise in this process – and in similar ones in other countries as well – if and whenever asked to do so, as and when the need should arise. Such needs may well proliferate in coming years. Commenting on Jacques Delors's thoughts on the options for the future relations of the GDR with the European Community,[21] and developing further his own ideas on a Greater Europe, the West German Foreign Minister Hans-Dietrich Genscher suggested in January 1990 that 'confederations and federations will determine the future picture of Europe'.[22] This would seem to be a prophecy on which future decisions can indeed be built.

Notes

1. This chapter is only able to take into account events and developments which took place up to the first free elections in the GDR on 18 March 1990.
2. See Friedrich-Ebert-Stiftung (ed.), *Zur Geschichte der DDR – von Ulbricht zu Honecker*, Bonn (1966), 36–42. Although the East German *Länder* were abolished in 1952, the *Länderkammer* was not formally dissolved until 1958. Up to this point, it was an elected assembly representing the new District Councils.
3. *Bundesrats-Drucksache 732/89* (Berlin, Bremen, North-Rhine-Westphalia, Saarland and Schleswig-Holstein); *Bundesrats-Drucksache 726/89* (Baden-Württemberg, Bavaria, Lower Saxony and Rhineland-Palatinate); *Bundesrats-Drucksache 737/89* (Hamburg); *Plenarprotokolle des Bundesrates* (1989), 559–85, 599–600.
4. *Plenarprotokolle des Bundesrates* (1990), 1–25.
5. *Bundesrats-Drucksache 105/90.*
6. *Bundestags-Drucksache 11/6462.*
7. See the wording of its second sentence, as reprinted in the Appendix to this volume.
8. Consensus on this issue grew only gradually and amid considerable controversy in January and February 1990. A great deal of confusion, which helped to fire the controversy, was created by the idea favoured by some CDU/CSU politicians that the right of accession under Article 23 could and should be exercised not by the GDR as a whole, but individually by the East German *Länder* (as soon as they were re-established). Such a procedure would inevitably have created severe constitutional and political problems, not just in West and East Germany but also in the international arena, since each individual act of accession would have required the consent of the post-war occupying powers (as would a single act of accession of the GDR as a whole). For the rights of the United States, France and the United Kingdom on this matter, see Article 2 of the Convention on Relations between the Three Powers and the Federal Republic of Germany, in

Bundesgesetzblatt II (1956), 218. The only occasion on which Article 23 has been employed before now was the accession of the Saarland to the Federal Republic on 1 January 1957.

9. The so-called 'Round Table' in East Berlin (which grew into the role of a political steering committee for the GDR from November 1989 up to the elections of 18 March 1990) discussed such territorial reforms, but, unfortunately, did not publish the suggestions presented to it.

10. See, 'Ausschuss zur Vereinigung Berlins', *Frankfurter Allgemeine Zeitung*, 22 March 1990.

11. See 'Engholm schlägt einen neuen Nordstaat vor', *Die Welt*, 2 March 1990.

12. See 'Zersplitterung im Auge', *Die Welt*, 23 December 1989.

13. 357,042 km².

14. United States (excluding Alaska) – 7,844,323 km²; Canada – 9,976,139 km²; Brazil – 8,511,965 km²; Australia – 7,686,844 km².

15. A united Germany would have a population density of 221 inhabitants/km², as compared with the United States (excluding Alaska, 31/km²), Canada (3/km²), Brazil (16/km²) and Australia (2/km²).

16. See Alfred Kubel, 'Bewährungen und Versäumnisse im Bundesstaat', in Rudolf Hrbek (ed.), *Miterlebt – Mitgestaltet. Der Bundesrat im Rückblick*, Bonn Aktuell, Stuttgart (1989), 50–64. See further in Chapters 3 and 7 of this volume.

17. After North-Rhine-Westphalia (17.1 m.), Bavaria (11.2 m.), Baden-Württemberg (9.6 m.), Lower Saxony (7.3 m.) and Hesse (5.7 m.).

18. See Albrecht, 'Bundeslander neu gliedern', *Frankfurter Allgemeine Zeitung*, 21 March 1990.

19. See the text of Article 29 in the Appendix to this volume.

20. Article 104a, Section 3 of the Basic Law.

21. These included independent accession, interim association or joining through accession to the Federal Republic under Article 23 of the Basic Law. See *Süddeutsche Zeitung*, 13 and 14 January 1990, and *Frankfurter Allgemeine Zeitung*, 13 January 1990.

22. Quoted in 'Die EC eröffnet "Beitrittsperspektiven" für die DDR', *Frankfurter Allgemeine Zeitung*, 13 January 1990.

Appendix:
Federalism in the Basic Law
Compiled by Uwe Leonardy

This Appendix is intended primarily as a source of reference for the Articles of the Basic Law which are mentioned in Chapters 3 and 8 of this volume. It also serves, of course, as a wider guide to constitutional aspects of the German federal structure, which will be of use as a source of reference for the other chapters in the volume. The English translation is taken from *Basic Law of the Federal Republic of Germany – promulgated by the Parliamentary Council on 23rd May 1949 as amended up to and including 21st December 1983*, published (and reprinted with the permission of) the Press and Information Office of the Federal Government, Bonn (1989). For reasons of space, any non-constitutional rules concerning German federalism cannot be included in the Appendix. For other legal sources on the subject, see *Handbuch des Bundesrates für das Geschäftsjahr 1989/90*.

II. THE FEDERATION AND THE STATES (LAENDER)

Article 20 (Basic principles of state order, right to resist)
(1) The Federal Republic of Germany shall be a democratic and social federal state.
. . .

Article 23 (Jurisdiction of the Basic Law)
For the time being, this Basic Law shall apply in the territory of the Laender of Baden**, Bavaria, Bremen, Greater Berlin, Hamburg, Hesse, Lower Saxony, North Rhine-Westphalia, Rhineland-Palatinate, Schleswig-Holstein, Wuerttemberg-Baden** and Wuerttemberg-Hohenzollern**. In other parts of Germany it shall be put into force on their accession***.

** By federal statute of 4 May 1951 (Federal Law Gazette I p. 284), the Land of Baden-Wuerttemberg was created out of the former Leander of Baden, Wuerttemberg-Baden and Wuerttemberg-Hohenzollern.

*** This Basic Law became effective in the Saarland by virtue of paragraph (1) of section 1 of the federal statute of 23 December 1956 (Federal Law Gazette I p. 1011).

Article 24 (Transfer of sovereign powers etc.)

(1) The Federation may by legislation transfer sovereign powers to intergovernmental institutions.

. . .

Article 28 (Federal guarantee of Laender constitutions, guarantee of self-government for local authorities)

(1) The constitutional order in the Laender shall conform to the principles of republican, democratic and social government based on the rule of law, within the meaning of this Basic Law. In each of the Laender, counties (Kreise), and communes (Gemeinden), the people shall be represented by a body chosen in general, direct, free, equal and secret elections. In the communes the communal assembly may take the place of an elected body.

(2) The communes shall be guaranteed the right to regulate, on their own responsibility, all the affairs of the local community within the limits set by statute. Within the framework of their statutory functions, the associations of communes (Gemeindeverbaende) shall also have such right of self-government as may be provided by statute.

(3) The Federation shall ensure that the constitutional order of the Laender conforms to the basic rights and to the provisions of paragraphs (1) and (2) of this Article.

Article 29* (New delimitation of Laender boundaries)

(1) A new delimitation of federal territory may be made to ensure that the Laender by their size and capacity are able effectively to fulfil the functions incumbent upon them. Due regard shall be given to regional, historical and cultural ties, economic expediency, regional policy, and the requirements of town and country planning.

(2) Measures for a new delimitation of federal territory shall be effected by federal statutes which shall require confirmation by referendum. The Laender thus affected shall be consulted.

(3) A referendum shall be held in the Laender from whose territories or partial territories a new Land or a Land with redefined boundaries is to be formed (affected Laender). The referendum shall be held on the question whether the affected Laender are to remain within their existing boundaries or whether the new Land or Land with redefined boundaries should be formed. The referendum shall be deemed to be in favour of the formation of a new Land or of a Land with redefined boundaries where approval is given to the change by a majority in the future territory of such Land and by a majority in all the

territories or partial territories of an affected Land whose assignments to a Land is to be changed in the same sense. The referendum shall be deemed not to be in favour where in the territory of one of the affected Laender a majority reject the change; such rejection shall, however, be of no consequence where in one part of the territory whose assignment to the affected Land is to be changed a majority of two-thirds approve of the change, unless in the entire territory of the affected Land a majority of two-thirds reject the change.

(4) Where in a clearly definable area of interconnected population and economic settlement, the parts of which lie in several Laender and which has a population of at least one million, one tenth of those of its population entitled to vote in Bundestag elections petition by popular initiative for the assignment of that area to one Land, provision shall be made within two years in a federal statute determining whether the delimitation of the affected Laender shall be changed pursuant to paragraph (2) of this Article or determining that a plebiscite shall be held in the affected Laender.

(5) The plebiscite shall establish whether approval is given to a change of Laender delimitation to be proposed in the statute. The statute may put forward different proposals, not exceeding two in number, for the plebiscite. Where approval is given by a majority to a proposed change of Laender delimitation, provision shall be made within two years in a federal statute determining whether the delimitation of the Laender concerned shall be changed pursuant to paragraph (2) of this Article. Where approval is given, in accordance with the third and fourth sentences of paragraph (3) of this Article, to a proposal put forward for the plebiscite, a federal statute providing for the formation of the proposed Land shall be enacted within two years of the plebiscite and shall no longer require confirmation by referendum.

(6) A majority in a referendum or in a plebiscite shall consist of a majority of the votes cast, provided that they amount to at least one quarter of the population entitled to vote in Bundestag elections. Other detailed provisions concerning referendums, popular petitions and plebiscites (Volksentscheide, Volksbegehren, Volksbefragungen) shall be made in a federal statute; such statute may also provide that popular petitions may not be repeated within a period of five years.

(7) Other changes concerning the territory of the Laender may be effected by state agreements between the Laender concerned or by a federal statute with the approval of the Bundesrat where the territory which is to be the subject of a new delimitation does not have more than 10,000 inhabitants. Detailed provision shall be made in a federal statute requiring the approval of the Bundesrat and the majority of the members of the Bundestag. It shall make provision for the affected communes and districts to be heard.

---

* As amended by federal statutes of 19 August 1969 (Federal Law Gazette I p. 1241) and of 23 August 1976 (Federal Law Gazette I p. 2381).

Article 30 (Distribution of competence between the Federation and the Laender)
Except as otherwise provided or permitted by this Basic Law, the exercise of governmental powers and the discharge of governmental functions shall be incumbent on the Leander.

. . .

Article 32 (Foreign relations)
(1) Relations with foreign states shall be conducted by the Federation.
(2) Before the conclusion of a treaty affecting the special circumstances of a Land, that Land shall be consulted in sufficient time.
(3) Insofar as the Laender have power to legislate, they may, with the consent of the Federal Government, conclude treaties with foreign states.

. . .

Article 36 (Personnel of the federal authorities)
(1) Civil servants employed in the highest federal authorities shall be drawn from all Laender in appropriate proportion. Persons employed in other federal authorities should, as a rule, be drawn from the Land in which they serve.
(2)** Military laws shall, inter alia, take into account both the division of the Federation into Laender and the regional ties of their populations.

**Inserted by federal statute of 19 March 1956 (Federal Law Gazette I p. 111).

Article 37 (Federal coercion)
(1) Where a Land fails to comply with its obligations of a federal character imposed by this Basic Law or another federal statute, the Federal Government may, with the consent of the Bundesrat, take the necessary measures to enforce such compliance by the Land by way of federal coercion.
(2) For the purpose of exercising such federal coercion, the Federal Government or its commissioner shall have the right to give instructions to all Laender and their authorities.

III. THE FEDERAL PARLIAMENT (BUNDESTAG)

Article 43 (Presence of members of the Federal Government and of the Bundesrat)
. . .
(2) The members of the Bundesrat and of the Federal Government as well as persons commissioned by them shall have access to all meetings of the Bundestag and its committees. They shall have the right to be heard at any time.

IV. THE FEDERAL COUNCIL (BUNDESRAT)

Article 50 (Functions)
The Laender shall participate through the Bundesrat in the legislation and administration of the Federation.

Article 51 (Composition)
(1) The Bundesrat shall consist of members of the Land governments which appoint and recall them. Other members of such governments may act as substitutes.
(2) Each Land shall have at least three votes; Laender with more than two million inhabitants shall have four, Laender with more than six million inhabitants five votes.
(3) Each Land may delegate as many members as it has votes. The votes of each Land may be cast only as a block vote and only by members present or their substitutes.

Article 52 (President, rules of procedure)
(1) The Bundesrat shall elect its President for one year.
(2) The President shall convene the Bundesrat. He shall convene the Bundesrat where delegates from at least two Laender or the Federal Government so demand.
(3) The Bundesrat shall take its decisions with at least the majority of its votes. It shall draw up its rules of procedure. Its meetings shall be public. The public may be excluded.
(4) Other members of or persons commissioned by Land governments may serve on the committees of the Bundesrat.

Article 53 (Presence of members of the Federal Government)
The members of the Federal Government shall have the right, and on demand the duty, to attend the meetings of the Bundesrat and of its committees. They shall have the right to be heard at any time. The Bundesrat shall be kept informed by the Federal Government as regards the conduct of affairs.

VII. LEGISLATIVE POWERS OF THE FEDERATION

Article 70 (Legislation of the Federation and the Laender)
(1) The Laender shall have the right to legislate insofar as this Basic Law does not confer legislative power on the Federation.
(2) The division of competence between the Federation and the Laender shall be determined by the provisions of this Basic Law concerning exclusive and concurrent legislative powers.

Article 71 (Exclusive legislative power of the Federation, definition)
In matters within the exclusive legislative power of the Federation, the Laender shall have power to lesiglate only where and to the extent that they are given such explicit authorization by a federal statute.

Article 72 (Concurrent legislative power of the Federation, definition)
(1) In matters within the concurrent legislative power, the Laender shall have power to legislate as long as and to the extent that the Federation does not exercise its right to legislate.
(2) The Federation shall have the right to legislate in these matters to the extent that a need for regulation by federal legislation exists because:
1. a matter cannot be effectively regulated by the legislation of individual Laender, or
2. the regulation of a matter by a Land statute might prejudice the interests of other Laender or of the people as a whole, or
3. the maintenance of legal or economic unity, especially the maintenance of uniformity of living conditions beyond the territory of any one Land, necessitates such regulation.

Article 73 (Exclusive legislative power, catalogue)
The Federation shall have exclusive power to legislate in the following matters:
1. *foreign affairs and defence, including the protection of the civilian population;
2. citizenship in the Federation;
3. freedom of movement, passport matters, immigration, emigration and extradition;
4. currency, money and coinage, weights and measures, as well as the determination of standards of time;
5. the unity of the customs and trading area, treaties on commerce and on navigation, the freedom of movement of goods, and the exchange of goods and payments with foreign countries, including customs and other frontier protection;
6. federal railroads and air transport;
7. postal and telecommunication services;
8. the legal status of persons employed by the Federation and by federal corporate bodies under public law;
9. industrial property rights, copyrights and publishing law;
10. *cooperation between the Federation and the Laender concerning
    (a) criminal police,
    (b) protection of the free democratic basic order, of the existence and the security of the Federation or of a Land (protection of the constitution) and
    (c) protection against activities in the federal territory which, through the use of force or actions in preparation for the use of force, endanger the foreign interests of the Federal Republic of Germany, as well as the

establishment of a Federal Criminal Police Office and the international control of crime;
11. statistics for federal purposes.

---

*As amended by federal statutes of 26 March 1954 (Federal Law Gazette I p. 45) and 24 June 1968 (Federal Law Gazette I p. 711).

Article 74 (Concurrent legislation, catalogue)
Concurrent legislative powers shall cover the following matters:
1. civil law, criminal law and execution of sentences, the organization and procedure of courts, the legal profession, notaries and legal advice (Rechtsberatung);
2. registration of births, deaths and marriages;
3. the law of association and assembly;
4. the law relating to residence and settlement of aliens;
4a.** the law relating to weapons and explosives;
5. the protection of German cultural assets against migration abroad;
6. refugee and expellee matters;
7. public welfare;
8. citizenship in the Laender;
9. war damage and reparations;
10.* benefits to war-disabled persons and to dependents of those killed in the war as well as assistance to former prisoners of war;
10a.** war graves of soldiers, graves of other victims of war and of victims of despotism;
11. the law relating to economic matters (mining, industry, supply of power, crafts, trades, commerce, banking, stock exchanges and private insurance);
11a.*** the production and utilization of nuclear energy for peaceful purposes, the construction and operation of installations serving such purposes, protection against hazards arising from the release of nuclear energy or from ionizing radiation, and the disposal of radioactive substances;
12. labour law, including the legal organization of enterprises, protection of workers, employment exchanges and agencies, as well as social insurance, including unemployment insurance;
13.**** the regulation of educational and training grants and the promotion of scientific research;
14. the law regarding expropriation, to the extent that matters enumerated in Articles 73 and 74 are concerned;
15. transfer of land, natural resources and means of production to public ownership or other forms of collective enterprise for the public benefit;
16. prevention of the abuse of economic power;
17. promotion of agricultural production and forestry, securing the supply of food, the importation and exportation of agricultural and forestry products, deep-sea and coastal fishing, and preservation of the coasts;
18. real estate transactions, land law and matters concerning agricultural leases, as well as housing, settlement and homestead matters;

156 UWE LEONARDY

19. measures against human and animal diseases that are communicable or otherwise endanger public health, admission to the medical profession and to the other medical occupations or practices, as well as trade in medicines, curatives, narcotics and poisons;

19a.* the economic viability of hospitals and the regulation of hospitalization fees;

20.** protection regarding the marketing of food, drink and tobacco, of necessities of life, fodder, agricultural and forest seeds and seedlings, and protection of plants against diseases and pests, as well as the protection of animals;

21. ocean and coastal shipping, as well as sea marks, inland navigation, meteorological services, sea routes, and inland waterways used for general traffic;

22.*** road traffic, motor transport, construction and maintenance of long distance highways, as well as the collection of charges for the use of public highways by vehicles and the allocation of revenue therefrom;

23. non-federal railroads, except mountain railroads;

24.**** waste disposal, air purification and noise abatement.

42.** Inserted by federal stature of 28 July 1972 (Federal Law Gazette I p. 1305) and amended by federal statute of 23 August 1976 (Federal Law Gazette I p. 2383).
10.* As amended by federal statute of 16 June 1965 (Federal Law Gazette I p. 513).
10.a.** Inserted by federal statute of 16 June 1965 (Federal Law Gazette I p. 513).
11.a.*** Inserted by federal statute of 23 December 1959 (Federal Law Gazette I p. 813).
13.**** As amended by federal statute of 12 May 1969 (Federal Law Gazette I p. 363).
19.a.* Inserted by federal statute of 12 May 1969 (Federal Law Gazette I p. 363).
20.** As amended by federal statute of 18 March 1971 (Federal Law Gazette I p. 207).
22.*** As amended by federal statute of 12 May 1969 (Federal Law Gazette I p. 363).
24.**** As amended by federal statute of 12 April 1971 (Federal Law Gazette I p. 593).

Article 74a* (Concurrent legislative power of the Federation, remuneration and pensions of members of the public service)

(1) Concurrent legislative power shall further extend to the remuneration and pensions of members of the public service whose service and loyalty are governed by public law, insofar as the Federation does not have exclusive power to legislate pursuant to item 8 of Article 73.

(2) Federal statutes enacted pursuant to paragraph (1) of this Article shall require the consent of the Bundesrat.

(3) Federal statutes enacted pursuant to item 8 of Article 73 shall likewise require the consent of the Bundesrat, insofar as for the structure and assessment of remuneration and pensions, including the rating of posts, provision is made for criteria or minimum or maximum rates other than those provided for in federal statutes enacted pursuant to paragraph (1) of this Article.

(4) Paragraphs (1) and (2) of this Article shall apply mutatis mutandis to the remuneration and pensions of judges in the Laender. Paragraph (3) of this Article shall apply mutatis mutandis to statutes enacted pursuant to paragraph (1) of Article 98.

---

*Inserted by federal statute of 18 March 1971 (Federal Law Gazette I p. 206).

Article 75* (Power of the Federation to pass outlining legislation, catalogue)
Subject to the conditions laid down in Article 72, the Federation shall have the right to enact outline provisions concerning:
1.** the legal status of persons in the public service of the Laender, communes or other corporate bodies under public law, insofar as Article 74a does not provide otherwise;
1a.*** the general principles governing higher education;
2. the general legal status of the press and the film industry;
3. hunting, nature conservation and landscape management;
4. land distribution, regional planning and the management of water resources;
5. matters relating to the registration of residence or domicile (Meldewesen) and to identity cards.

---

*As amended by federal statute of 12 May 1969 (Federal Law Gazette I p. 363).
**As amended by federal statute of 18 March 1971 (Federal Law Gazette I p. 206).
***Inserted by federal statute of 12 May 1969 (Federal Law Gazette I p. 363).

Article 76 (Bills)
(1) Bills shall be introduced in the Bundestag by the Federal Government or by members of the Bundestag or by the Bundesrat.
(2) Bills of the Federal Government shall first be submitted to the Bundesrat. The Bundesrat shall be entitled to state its position on such bills within six weeks. A bill which, on submission to the Bundesrat, is exceptionally specified by the Federal Government to be particularly urgent may be submitted by the latter to the Bundestag three weeks later, even though the Federal Government may not yet have received the statement of the Bundesrat's position; upon receipt, such statement shall be transmitted to the Bundestag by the Federal Government without delay.
(3)* Bills of the Bundesrat shall be submitted to the Bundestag by the Federal Government within three months. In doing so, the Federal Government shall ͻͻate its own view.

---

*As amended by federal statute of 15 November 1968 (Federal Law Gazette I p. 1177).
*As amended by federal statute of 17 July 1969 (Federal Law Gazette I p. 817).

Article 77 (Legislative procedure)
(1) Federal statutes shall be enacted by the Bundestag. Upon their adoption they shall, without delay, be transmitted to the Bundesrat by the President of the Bundestag.
(2)** The Bundesrat may, within three weeks of the receipt of the adopted bill, demand that a committee for joint consideration of bills, composed of members of the Bundestag and members of the Bundesrat, be convened. The composition and the procedure of this committee shall be regulated by rules of procedure to be adopted by the Bundestag and requiring the consent of the Bundesrat. The

members of the Bundesrat on this committee shall not be bound by instructions. Where the consent of the Bundesrat is required for a bill to become a statute, the Bundestag and the Federal Government may also demand that the committee be convened. Should the committee propose any amendment to the adopted bill, the Bundestag shall again vote on the bill.

(3)** Insofar as the consent of the Bundesrat is not required for a bill to become a statute, the Bundesrat may, when the proceedings under paragraph (2) of this Article are completed, enter an objection within two weeks against a bill adopted by the Bundestag. The period for entering an objection shall begin, in the case of the last sentence of paragraph (2) of this Article, on the receipt of the bill as readopted by the Bundestag, and in all other cases on the receipt of a communication from the chairman of the committee provided for in paragraph (2) of this Article to the effect that the committee's proceedings have been concluded.

(4) Where the objection was adopted with the majority of the votes of the Bundesrat, it can be rejected by a decision of the majority of the members of the Bundestag. Where the Bundesrat adopted the objection with a majority of at least two thirds of its votes, its rejection by the Bundestag shall require a majority of two thirds, including at least the majority of the members of the Bundestag.

** As amended by federal statute of 15 November 1968 (Federal Law Gazette I p. 1177).

Article 78 (Passage of federal statutes)
A bill adopted by the Bundestag shall become a statute where the Bundesrat consents to it, or fails to make a demand pursuant to paragraph (2) of Article 77, or fails to enter an objection within the period stipulated in paragraph (3) of Article 77, or withdraws such objection, or where the objection is overridden by the Bundestag.

Article 79 (Amendment of the Basic Law)
(1) This Basic Law can be amended only by statutes which expressly amend or supplement the text thereof. In respect of international treaties, the subject of which is a peace settlement, the preparation of a peace settlement or the phasing out of an occupation regime, or which are intended to serve the defence of the Federal Republic, it shall be sufficient, for the purpose of clarifying that the provisions of this Basic Law do not preclude the conclusion and entry into force of such treaties, to effect a supplementation of the text of this Basic Law confined to such clarification*.

(2) Any such statute shall require the consent of two thirds of the members of the Bundestag and two thirds of the votes of the Bundesrat.

(3) Amendments of this Basic Law affecting the division of the Federation into Laender the participation on principle of the Laender in legislation, or the basic principles laid down in Articles 1 and 20 shall be inadmissible.

---

*Second sentence inserted by federal statute of 26 March 1954 (Federal Law Gazette I p. 45).

Article 80 (Issue of ordinances)

(1) The Federal Government, a Federal Minister or the Land governments may be authorized by statute to issue ordinances (Rechtsverordnungen). The content, purpose and scope of the authorization so conferred shall be laid down in the statute concerned. This legal basis shall be stated in the ordinance. Where a statute provides that such authorization may be delegated, such delegation shall require another ordinance.

(2) The consent of the Bundesrat shall be required, unless otherwise provided by federal legislation, for ordinances issued by the Federal Government or a Federal Minister concerning basic rules for the use of facilities of the federal railroads and of postal and telecommunication services, or charges therefor, or concerning the construction and operation of railroads, as well as for ordinances issued pursuant to federal statutes that require the consent of the Bundesrat or that are executed by the Laender as agents of the Federation or as matters of their own concern.

VII. THE EXECUTION OF FEDERAL STATUTES AND THE FEDERAL ADMINISTRATION

Article 83 (Distribution of competence between the Federation and the Laender)

The Laender shall execute federal statutes as matters of their own concern insofar as this Basic Law does not otherwise provide or permit.

Article 84 (Land execution and Federal Government supervision)

(1) Where the Laender execute federal statutes as matters of their own concern, they shall provide for the establishment of the requisite authorities and the regulation of administrative procedures insofar as federal statutes consented to by the Bundesrat do not otherwise provide.

(2) The Federal Government may, with the consent of the Bundesrat, issue pertinent general administrative rules.

(3) The Federal Government shall exercise supervision to ensure that the Laender execute the federal statutes in accordance with applicable law. For this purpose the Federal Government may send commissioners to the highest Land authorities and, with their consent or, where such consent is refused, with the consent of the Bundesrat, also to subordinate authorities.

(4) Should any shortcomings which the Federal Government has found to exist in the execution of federal statutes in the Laender not be corrected, the Bundesrat shall decide, at the request of the Federal Government or the Land concerned, whether such Land has violated the law. The decision of the Bundesrat may be challenged in the Federal Constitutional Court.

(5) With a view to the execution of federal statutes, the Federal Government may be authorized by a federal statute requiring the consent of the Bundesrat to issue individual instructions for particular cases. They shall be addressed to the

highest Land authorities unless the Federal Government considers the matter urgent.

Article 85 (Execution by the Laender as agents of the Federation)
(1) Where the Laender execute federal statutes as agents of the Federation, the establishment of the requisite authorities shall remain the concern of the Laender, except insofar as federal statutes consented to by the Bundesrat otherwise provide.
(2) The Federal Government may, with the consent of the Bundesrat, issue pertinent general administrative rules. It may regulate the uniform training of civil servants (Beamte) and other salaried public employees (Angestellte). The heads of authorities at the intermediate level shall be appointed with its agreement.
(3) The Land authorities shall be subject to the instructions of the appropriate highest federal authorities. Such instructions shall be addressed to the highest Land authorities unless the Federal Government considers the matter urgent. Execution of the instructions shall be ensured by the highest Land authorities.
(4) Federal supervision shall cover the lawfulness and appropriateness of execution. The Federal Government may, for this purpose, require the submission of reports and documents and send commissioners to all authorities.

Article 86 (Direct federal administration)
Where the Federation executes statutes by means of direct federal administration or by federal corporate bodies or institutions under public law, the Federal Government shall, insofar as the statute concerned contains no special provision, issue pertinent general administrative rules. The Federal Government shall provide for the establishment of the requisite authorities insofar as the statute concerned does not otherwise provide.

Article 87* (Matters for direct federal administration)
(1) The foreign service, the federal finance administration, the federal railroads, the federal postal service and, in accordance with the provisions of Article 89, the administration of federal waterways and of shipping shall be conducted as matters of direct federal administration with their own administrative substructures. Federal legislation may be enacted to establish Federal Border Guard authorities and central offices for police information and communications, for the criminal police and for the compilation of data for the purposes of protection of the constitution and of protection against activities on federal territory which, through the use of force or acts preparatory to the use of force, endanger the foreign interests of the Federal Republic of Germany.
(2) Social insurance institutions whose sphere of competence extends beyond the territory of one Land shall be administered as federal corporate bodies under public law.
(3) In addition, autonomous federal higher authorities as well as new federal corporate bodies and institutions under public law may be established by federal

legislation for matters on which the Federation has the power to legislate. Where new functions arise for the Federation in matters on which it has the power to legislate, federal authorities at the intermediate and lower levels may be established, in case of urgent need, with the consent of the Bundesrat and of the majority of the members of the Bundestag.

---

*Inserted by federal statute of 19 March 1956 (Federal Law Gazette I p. 111) and amended by federal statute of 24 June 1968 (Federal Law Gazette I p. 711).

Article 87b* (Administration of the Federal Armed Forces)
(1) The Federal Armed Forces Administration shall be conducted as a direct federal administration with its own administrative substructure. Its function shall be to administer personnel matters and directly to meet the material requirements of the Armed Forces. Tasks connected with benefits to injured persons or with construction work shall not be assigned to the Federal Armed Forces Administration except by federal legislation requiring the consent of the Bundesrat. Such consent shall also be required for any statutes to the extent that they empower the Federal Armed Forces Administration to interfere with rights of third parties; this shall, however, not apply in the case of statutes concerning personnel matters.
(2) Moreover, federal statutes concerning defence, including recruitment for military service and protection of the civilian population, may, with the consent of the Bundesrat, provide that they shall be executed, wholly or in part, either by means of direct federal administration having its own administrative substructure or by the Laender acting as agents of the Federation. Where such statutes are executed by the Laender acting as agents of the Federation, they may, with the consent of the Bundesrat, provide that the powers vested in the Federal Government or appropriate highest federal authorities by virtue of Article 85 shall be transferred wholly or in part to higher federal authorities; in such an event it may be enacted that these authorities shall not require the consent of the Bundesrat in issuing general administrative rules as referred to in the first sentence of paragraph (2) of Article 85.

---

*Inserted by federal statute of 19 March 1956 (Federal Law Gazette I p. 111).

Article 87c* (Delegated administration in the field of nuclear energy)
Statutes enacted under item 11a of Article 74 may, with the consent of the Bundesrat, provide that they shall be executed by the Laender acting as agents of the Federation.

---

*Inserted by federal statute of 23 December 1959 (Federal Law Gazette I p. 813).

Article 87d** (Aviation administration)
(1) Aviation administration shall be conducted as a direct federal administration.

(2) Through federal legislation requiring the consent of the Bundesrat, functions of aviation administration may be delegated to the Laender acting as agents of the Federation.

** Inserted by federal statute of 6 February 1961 (Federal Law Gazette I p. 65).

Article 89 (Federal waterways)

(1) The Federation shall be the owner of the former Reich waterways.

(2) The Federation shall administer the federal waterways through its own authorities. It shall exercise those governmental functions relating to inland shipping which extend beyond the territory of one Land, and those governmental functions relating to maritime shipping which are conferred on it by statute. Upon request, the Federation may transfer the administration of federal waterways, insofar as they lie within the territory of one Land, to that Land as its agent. Where a waterway touches the territories of several Laender, the Federation may delegate one Land to be its agent where so requested by the Laender concerned.

(3) In the administration, development and new construction of waterways, the needs of land improvement and of water economy shall be safeguarded in agreement with the Laender.

Article 90 (Federal highways)

(1) The Federation shall be the owner of the former Reich motorways (Reichsautobahnen) and Reich highways.

(2) The Laender, or such self-governing corporate bodies as are competent under Land law, shall administer as agents of the Federation the federal motorways and other federal highways used for long-distance traffic.

(3) At the request of a Land, the Federation may place federal motorways and other federal highways used for long-distance traffic under direct federal administration insofar as they lie within the territory of that Land.

VIIIa. JOINT TASKS*

Article 91a* (Participation of the Federation by virtue of federal legislation)

(1) The Federation shall participate, in the following sectors, in the discharge of responsibilities of the Laender, provided that such responsibilities are important to society as a whole and that federal participation is necessary for the improvement of living conditions (joint tasks):

1.** extension and construction of institutions of higher education, including university clinics;

2. improvement of regional economic structures;

3. improvement of the agrarian structure and of coast preservation.

(2) Joint tasks shall be defined in detail by a federal statute requiring the consent of the Bundesrat. Such legislation should include general principles governing the discharge of joint tasks.

(3) Such legislation shall provide for the procedure and the institutions required for joint overall planning. The inclusion of a project in the overall planning shall require the consent of the Land in which it is to be carried out.

(4) In cases to which items 1 and 2 of paragraph (1) of this Article apply, the Federation shall meet one half of the expenditure in each Land. In cases to which item 3 of paragraph (1) of this Article applies, the Federation shall meet at least one half of the expenditure, and such proportion shall be the same for all the Laender. Details shall be regulated by statute. Provision of funds shall be subject to appropriation in the budgets of the Federation and the Laender.

(5) The Federal Government and the Bundesrat shall be informed about the execution of joint tasks, should they so demand.

*Inserted by federal statute of 12 May 1969 (Federal Law Gazette I p. 359).
**As amended by federal statute of 31 July 1970 (Federal Law Gazette I p. 1161).

Article 91b* (Cooperation of the Federation and the Laender by virtue of agreements made)
The Federation and the Laender may, pursuant to agreements, cooperate in educational planning and in the promotion of institutions and projects of scientific research of supraregional importance. The apportionment of costs shall be regulated in the relevant agreements.

*Inserted by federal statute of 12 May 1969 (Federal Law Gazette I p. 359).

IX. THE ADMINISTRATION OF JUSTICE

Article 94 (Federal Constitutional Court, composition)
(1) The Federal Constitutional Court shall consist of federal judges and other members. Half of the members of the Federal Constitutional Court shall be elected by the Bundestag and half by the Bundesrat. They may not be members of the Bundestag, the Bundesrat, the Federal Government, nor of any of the corresponding bodies of a Land.

X. FINANCE

Article 104a* (Apportionment of expenditure between the Federation and the Laender)
. . .
(3) Federal statutes to be executed by the Laender and granting money payments may make provision for such payments to be met wholly or in part by the Federation. Where any such statute provides that the Federation shall meet one half of the expenditure or more, it shall be implemented by the Laender as agents of the Federation. Where any such statute provides that the Laender shall meet one quarter of the expenditure or more, it shall require the consent of the Bundesrat.

(4) The Federation may grant the Laender financial assistance for particularly important investments by the Laender or communes or associations of communes, provided that such investments are necessary to avert a disturbance of the overall economic equilibrium or to equalize differences of economic capacities within the federal territory or to promote economic growth. Details, especially concerned the kinds of investments to be promoted, shall be regulated by a federal statute requiring the consent of the Bundesrat or by administrative arrangements under the federal budget law.

. . .

Article 106*** (Apportionment of tax revenue)
. . .
(3) Revenue from income taxes, corporation taxes and turnover taxes shall accrue jointly to the Federation and the Laender (joint taxes) to the extent that the revenue from the income tax is not allocated to the communes pursuant to paragraph (5) of this Article. The Federation and the Laender shall share equally the revenues from income taxes and corporation taxes. The respective shares of the Federation and the Laender in the revenue from the turnover tax shall be determined by a federal state requiring the consent of the Bundesrat. Such determination shall be based on the following principles:
. . .
2.　The coverage requirements of the Federation and of the Laender shall be coordinated in such a way that a fair balance is struck, any overburdening of taxpayers precluded and uniformity of living standards in the federal territory ensured.
. . .

***As amended by federal statutes of 23 December 1955 (Federal Law Gazette I p. 817), of 24 December 1956 (Federal Law Gazette I p. 1077), and of 12 May 1969 (Federal Law Gazette I p. 359).

XI. TRANSITIONAL AND CONCLUDING PROVISIONS

Article 146 (Duration of validity of the Basic Law)
This Basic Law shall cease to be in force on the day on which a constitution adopted by a free decision of the German people comes into force.

Index